SAN FRANCISCO

By Geoffrey Moorhouse
and the Editors of Time-Life Books

Photographs by Jay Maisel

THE GREAT CITIES · TIME-LIFE BOOKS · AMSTERDAM

The Author: Geoffrey Moorhouse was born in Bolton, England, in 1931. After leaving school at 18 and serving in the Royal Navy, he became a journalist. For many years he was the chief features writer of *The Guardian*, a job that took him to 43 countries. His books include *Calcutta*—a vivid study of that city—and *The Fearful Void*, an account of his own 2,000-mile journey by camel across the Sahara desert, the longest solo passage of its kind by a European.

The Photographer: Jay Maisel was born in Brooklyn, New York, in 1931. He studied painting at Cooper Union Art School and at Yale University, where he switched to a career in photography. His pictures have appeared in numerous magazines and books including several volumes published by TIME-LIFE Books, the most recent being *Jerusalem* in *The Great Cities* series. He has also had many one-man exhibitions of his work.

TIME-LIFE INTERNATIONAL
EUROPEAN EDITOR: George Constable
Assistant European Editor: Kit van Tulleken
Design Consultant: Louis Klein
Chief Designer: Graham Davis
Director of Photography: Pamela Marke
Chief of Research: Vanessa Kramer

THE GREAT CITIES
Series Editor: Simon Rigge

Editorial Staff for San Francisco
Deputy Editor: Christopher Farman
Designers: Derek Copsey, Joyce Mason
Picture Editor: Christine Hinze
Staff Writer: Mike Brown
Text Researchers: Elizabeth Loving, Milly Trowbridge
Design Assistant: Mary Staples
Sub-editors: Ilse Gray (chief), Nicoletta Flessati

Editorial Production
Production Editor: Ellen Brush
Art Department: Julia West
Editorial Department: Joanne Holland, Ajaib Singh Gill
Picture Department: Stephanie Lindsay, Belinda Stewart Cox

The captions and the texts accompanying the photographs in this volume were prepared by the editors of TIME-LIFE Books.

Valuable assistance was given in the preparation of this volume by Janet Zich in San Francisco.

Published by TIME-LIFE Books (Nederland) B.V.
Ottho Heldringstraat 5, Amsterdam 1018.

ISBN 7054 0495 1

Cover: A section of the Golden Gate Bridge looms through the mist like a giant harp. The main span of the bridge stretches 4,200 feet across the entrance to San Francisco Bay—a length more than double that of any other suspension span in existence when the bridge was completed in 1937.

First end paper: Silhouetted against a golden evening sky, San Franciscans cross cable-car tracks on Nob Hill, the prestigious summit on which the city's 19th-Century railroad barons built their palatial homes.

Last end paper: Steel, weathered wood and fading yellow paint define the edge of a turntable in the powerhouse and repair shop for San Francisco's historic cable cars. The opening in the slot between the rails allows a grip mechanism to be raised above the constantly moving underground cable so that the grip can be checked for wear.

Contents

I

City of Golden Dreams

The best way to see San Francisco is from the top of a hill. Within the city limits, there are no fewer than 43 to choose from; but the one that is known as Twin Peaks, with two summits more than 900 feet above sea-level, offers the finest panorama of all. Stand on the viewing terrace at the top and you understand at once how geography has helped to make San Francisco a mythical place.

To the left, the Pacific pours into the land through the spectacular gap called the Golden Gate. That is where San Francisco Bay begins, though to call it a bay is to misuse a serviceable little word. There are more than 400 square miles of water inside the Golden Gate, an expanse that ranks as nothing less than an inland sea. This sea, nowhere measuring more than 13 miles from east to west, extends at least twice that distance north and south of the Gate. The northern end is called San Pablo Bay, and even from the height of Twin Peaks, it can be detected only on a very clear day. The water that faces you as you stand with your back to the Pacific is San Francisco Bay proper, with the cities of Richmond, Berkeley and Oakland streaming along the eastern shore. Below Twin Peaks, as though at the centre of a stupendous amphitheatre, lies San Francisco itself.

Market Street, emerging from a nervous system of downtown sky-scrapers, runs straight and wide towards you, a vital artery of commerce and big business. The area to its right is the nearest San Francisco ever gets to being an ordinary city: suburbs, interrupted by blotches of derelict land, dribble south along the shore of the Bay, past Candlestick Park—the windiest baseball stadium in the United States—and out towards the international airport. To the left of Market Street are the districts that have given the name of San Francisco such a lyrical ring. Here are Telegraph Hill and Nob Hill, Chinatown and North Beach, Fisherman's Wharf and the Haight district. Surveyed from this vantage point on Twin Peaks, it all cascades beneath you in undulating terraces and parklands, in metro-politan leaps and bounds.

The hills of San Francisco help to maintain both native and visitor in quite remarkable states of euphoria, for no one can travel very far without being presented with a view that is at least interesting. Get someone to drive you along any street running north of Market and sooner or later you will top a hill high enough and steep enough to offer the illusion that you are about to take off into space and splash down into the Bay some-where just short of Alcatraz Island. It doesn't matter how many times you repeat this exercise and are instantly assured that the street continues

The setting sun burnishes a group of office blocks in downtown San Francisco, leaving the towering slab of the Bank of America and its pyramidal neighbour, headquarters of the Transamerica Corporation, in shadow. The buildings stand on the site of the old commercial centre, an area that was almost completely levelled in the 1906 earthquake.

down a couple of miles further before reaching the water: your breath is always taken away by the experience. And if you head downtown from the western side of the city, eventually you will seem to be dive-bombing the foundations of the skyscrapers.

It doesn't do, of course, to linger over these impressions if you are sitting in the driver's seat yourself. You have much to concentrate on when driving up and down San Francisco's hills, which are so steep in places—and so abundant whatever their gradient—that San Francisco has devised a special signpost that intones on the ups and downs like a litany: "Prevent Runaways. Curb Wheels. Park in Gear. Set Brake." And parking is indeed a challenge when you have to struggle not only with a tight space, but with a feeling of being half way to heaven or hell. At first glance, it would seem that residents whose steep streets are wide enough for angle parking have it best. But one of them swore to me that once, in a high wind, his car was blown over on to the car just downhill— and I can almost believe it.

Presently, however, a driver becomes accustomed to travelling the hills of San Francisco, learning to take his foot off the accelerator at precisely the right moment before topping the rise, so that he doesn't either shoot wildly over the top or, more miserably, stall and roll back. When he masters that skill, he invariably feels confident enough to tackle the stretch of Lombard Street between Leavenworth and Hyde. Commonly called "the crookedest street in the world", it has eight switchbacks in the space of a couple of hundred yards; the motorist should attempt it only at walking speed, if he is not to finish up in some helpless householder's front window.

The hills not only lift the spirit of San Franciscans, but do their constitutions a power of good as well. Much of the population must spend a fair amount of time walking up and down those hills, if only to get home from the nearest bus-stop or cable-car stage. And for many other residents, the hills are there to be taken at a run—or at least a healthy jog. Jogging is something of an obsession in this city, for almost all ages and both sexes, and you can come across a jogger at any hour of day or night. When I lived on Chestnut Street, an elderly gent used to pound the pavements of Telegraph Hill every morning before dawn, making me deeply ashamed that I was only exercising my eyes on the speckle of lights around the Bay. At the close of any workday, take a stroll towards Fort Point— where a 19th-Century bastion guards the Golden Gate—and a succession of joggers will patter past, touch wall at the fort, and return whence they came, in the direction of the city centre nearly four miles away.

Some joggers clearly feel they aren't giving themselves their money's worth just by moving doggedly from one place to another. I have seen the most inoffensive-looking people shadow-boxing like pugs as they run. But my favourite cameo remains that of two men I saw twirling around Golden Gate Park together, crossing and recrossing each other's paths

A Victorian wood-framed house, boarded up and blank except for a humorously painted top window, awaits removal to a new site. San Franciscans take endless trouble to preserve mementoes of their 19th-Century past, when most houses were built of wood—one reason why the city burned down, wholly or in part, six times in its early rip-roaring days and suffered so badly in the holocaust of 1906.

An aerial view captures the city's spectacular setting. To the left is Golden Gate Bridge, to the right the Embarcadero, and north across the Bay, Marin County.

(and sometimes running backwards for a change) like a pair of windblown leaves. Somehow, San Franciscans manage to elevate the laborious old art of footslogging from the merely pedestrian to the positively racy, and it obviously keeps a lot of them in pretty good trim.

The only thing I have against the hills of San Francisco is that they cause you to linger too long at their summits, if you get half a chance, when you should be going about your business. Those sweeping prospects of the Bay are too seductive for anyone who is naturally pensive. Even on a gloomy day in winter, when rain sags over the Golden Gate Bridge and obscures most of the distant shores, you can lose a whole hour contemplating the way some trick of light has left the cliffs and the abandoned island prison of Alcatraz in the middle of the Bay luminous in the haze—a glowing vision that a painter might try for a lifetime to catch. But, then, this bay has always been an inspiration of dreamers, beginning with the Spanish adventurers who settled California in the 18th Century. Many other cities, in the Old World as well as in the New, have been founded by visionaries, but succeeding generations are apt to settle for a viable lifestyle that lies between an ideal and disillusionment. What distinguishes San Francisco is that here people have not yet stopped imagining a more perfect future; the baton of optimism has been passed on faithfully from one generation to the next; and though there may have been fumbling at times, nobody has actually dropped the thing yet.

I cannot claim this as a new thought, for it has been codified in oil paint on top of Nob Hill. There, in the very posh Mark Hopkins Hotel, is a rather forbidding reception area called (after the Spanish title for grandees) the Room of the Dons. A series of murals decorates its walls: a cluster of Indians here, a handful of sailors there, an imperious Spanish aristocrat by the mantelpiece and breastplated soldiery all over the place—the entire lot standing against a background (excessive to my mind) of gold leaf. The two artists who painted the murals in the 1920s named the work "Golden Dreams". This title was intended to convey their feelings about the history and promise of California as a whole. But nowhere in the state—not even in Los Angeles, where dreams are packaged for the whole world—is it a more valid statement than in San Francisco.

The first of the dreamers to come wandering up this foggy and rugged coast were a pair of Portuguese sea captains in the pay of Spain, seeking the fabled Northwest Passage, thought to link the Atlantic and Pacific Oceans. In 1542, Juan Rodriguez Cabrillo sailed right past San Francisco Bay without noticing it, and a year later Bartolomé Ferrelo did the same. The next known European to arrive was Francis Drake, who also missed the narrow gap of the Golden Gate in 1579. But Drake did land 50 miles to the north and, calling the land "Nova Albion", annexed it to the British Crown. According to a long-disputed version of California's history, he is said to have tacked a brass plate to a wooden post on the shore, with the legend "Bee it known unto all men by these presents . . . I take possession of this kingdome . . ." The plate was found by a roadside in 1933 and is exhibited, all tarnished and scratched, in the University of California's Bancroft Library. If genuine, it is the area's oldest archaeological trophy from Europe, but ever since its discovery it has been regarded by some scholars as a forgery, and the latest laboratory tests on the composition of the brass support this view.

A few years after Drake's visit, the Spanish sea captain Sebastian Cermeño found himself shipwrecked in 1595 close to the spot where the Englishman had staked the first claim. Cermeño promptly annexed the land in the name of his own king. He called it Puerto de San Francisco, in honour of St. Francis of Assisi, then sailed away to Mexico in the ship's launch, which had survived undamaged.

It was not until the late-18th Century that Spaniards discovered the elusive bay and started a settlement there. Their New World empire was well-established by then, with a viceroy in Mexico City, and in a new spirit of expansion they were beginning to extend their territories to the north. As part of this policy, an expedition led by Don Gaspar de Portolá travelled up the coast overland and, in November 1769, reached the inland sea for the first time. Actually, Portolá himself never saw the bay. A scouting party under a non-commissioned officer, Sergeant José Francisco de Ortega, made the find; and the only description of the discovery was written second-hand by the expedition's padre, Juan Crespi, who remained with the main party. The scouts had seen, he tells us, "an immense arm of the sea, or an estuary, which penetrated the land as far as the eye could reach". The entire expedition, beset by hunger and illness, retreated south without investigating further.

But the Spanish interest was thoroughly aroused when Portolá and his men reached their base in San Diego and made their report. No one was more eager for that "immense arm of the sea" to be properly explored than Padre Junipero Serra, Father Superior of the Franciscan friars in California, whose religious order had started to build a long chain of mission stations up the coast from the south. Anxious to add to that chain and to win yet more Indian souls to the Catholic faith, he sent out a new party, 14-men strong and led by Pedro Fages and Padre Crespi. They started from the mission at Carmel in the spring of 1772 to look for a new site on the shores of the bay. Arriving on the hills where Berkeley now stands, the missionaries were the first Europeans to look out to the Pacific through the famous gap in the cliffs at the Golden Gate. Then they, too, returned to their base in the south.

When the party confirmed that the inland sea could be reached from the ocean, the viceroy in Mexico City despatched Lieutenant Juan Manuel de Ayala in the ship *San Carlos* to investigate further. On

Pride of the Bay

Located 350 miles north-west of Los Angeles on America's West Coast, San Francisco occupies a stubby peninsula bounded by the Pacific Ocean, San Francisco Bay and the two-mile-wide gap of the Golden Gate, where the waters meet. The city got its start in the 18th Century as a Spanish outpost, fell into U.S. hands in 1846 and promptly exploded in size and vigour when gold was discovered two years later at nearby Coloma (inset map, right). Later, Nevada silver, Pacific shipping and the first transcontinental railroad helped keep the city rich. Today, a host of other communities are prospering around the 450-square-mile Bay (inset map, below), but San Francisco—abounding in parks (green areas), spectacular views from its 43 hills (beige areas), and a still-venturesome spirit—remains the region's spiritual hub.

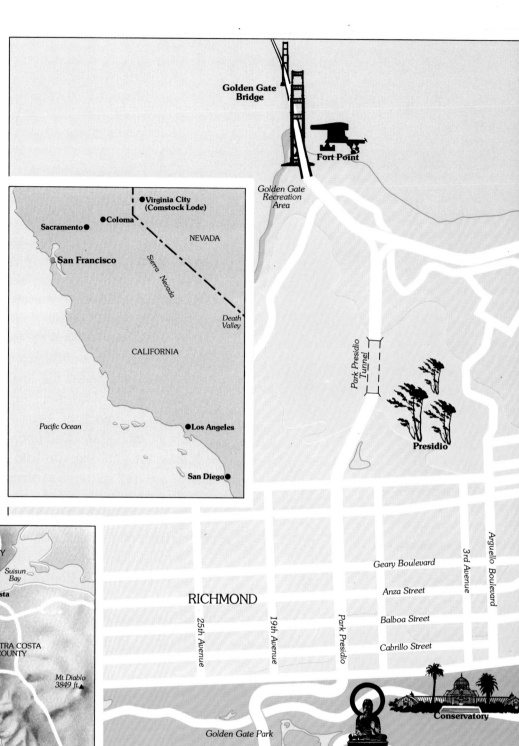

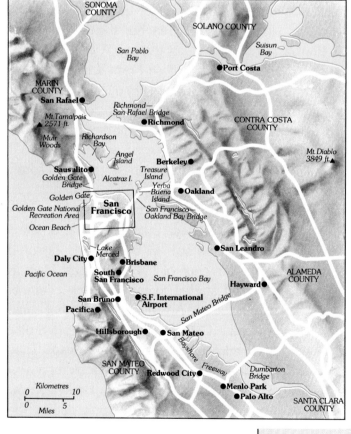

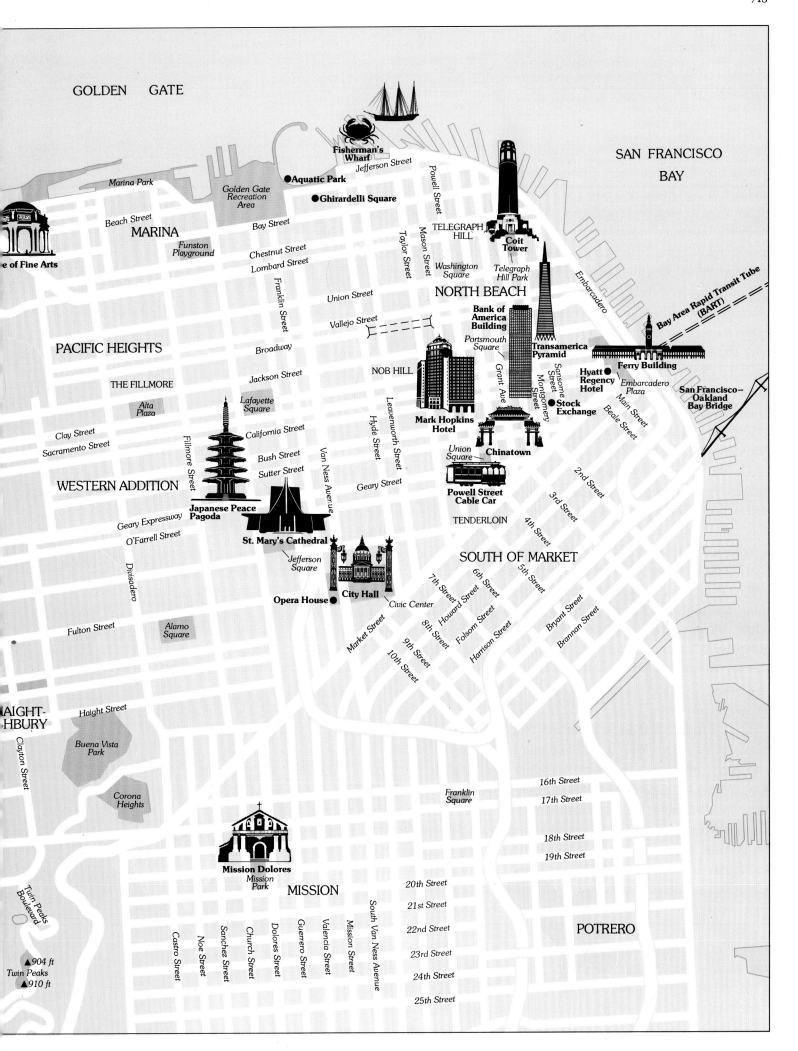

GOLDEN GATE

SAN FRANCISCO BAY

Fisherman's Wharf

Jefferson Street

●Aquatic Park

●Ghirardelli Square

Marina Park

Golden Gate Recreation Area

Beach Street

MARINA

Funston Playground

Bay Street

Chestnut Street

Lombard Street

e of Fine Arts

Powell Street

TELEGRAPH HILL

Coit Tower

Mason Street

Taylor Street

Washington Square

Telegraph Hill Park

NORTH BEACH

Embarcadero

Bay Area Rapid Transit Tube (BART)

Union Street

Vallejo Street

Bank of America Building

Transamerica Pyramid

PACIFIC HEIGHTS

Broadway

Franklin Street

Jackson Street

Portsmouth Square

Grant Ave

Sansome Street

Montgomery Street

Hyatt Regency Hotel ●

Ferry Building

NOB HILL

THE FILLMORE

Alta Plaza

Lafayette Square

California Street

Mark Hopkins Hotel

Embarcadero Plaza

San Francisco–Oakland Bay Bridge

● Stock Exchange

Clay Street

Sacramento Street

Bush Street

Sutter Street

Fillmore Street

Leavenworth Street

Hyde Street

Union Square

Chinatown

Main Street

Beale Street

WESTERN ADDITION

Japanese Peace Pagoda

Geary Street

Powell Street Cable Car

2nd Street

Geary Expressway

O'Farrell Street

Van Ness Avenue

TENDERLOIN

3rd Street

4th Street

St. Mary's Cathedral

Divisadero

Jefferson Square

SOUTH OF MARKET

5th Street

6th Street

Opera House ●

City Hall

Civic Center

7th Street

Howard Street

Folsom Street

Harrison Street

Bryant Street

Brannan Street

Fulton Street

Alamo Square

8th Street

9th Street

10th Street

Market Street

HAIGHT-
HBURY

Haight Street

Buena Vista Park

16th Street

17th Street

Clayton Street

Corona Heights

Franklin Square

18th Street

19th Street

Mission Dolores

Mission Park

MISSION

20th Street

21st Street

POTRERO

Twin Peaks Boulevard

▲904 ft
Twin Peaks
▲910 ft

Castro Street

Noe Street

Sanchez Street

Church Street

Dolores Street

Guerrero Street

Valencia Street

Mission Street

South Van Ness Avenue

22nd Street

23rd Street

24th Street

25th Street

August 5, 1775, the *San Carlos* sailed between the cliffs and dropped anchor in San Francisco Bay. Lieutenant de Ayala and his crew then spent more than a week cruising the local waters before beating a passage home with the fantastic news: "It is not a port," he reported, "but a whole pocketful of ports." He was to return the following year to lend a hand to the first band of settlers, who set out from Mexico in October, 1775.

Under the leadership of Captain Juan Bautista de Anza and Lieutenant José Moraga, 240 souls left Mexico. But when births and deaths *en route* were taken into account, settlers numbered 244 when they arrived in the bay the following summer. Apart from 40 families who would form the nucleus of the new colony, there were three officers and their victualler, three priests, 18 veteran soldiers and 20 recruits, 29 soldiers' wives plus their children, 20 muleteers, three cattle herdsmen, four servants for the priests and three Indian interpreters. The colonists also brought along a thousand head of cattle.

On June 29, 1776—just five days before the people on the opposite side of the continent were disassociating themselves from another empire with their Declaration of Independence—the imperial standard of Charles III of Spain was raised over the commander's quarters in the Presidio, the military garrison built among trees just inside the Golden Gate. Cannon fired exuberantly, a mass was said, and priests, settlers, sailors from the *San Carlos* and soldiery joined in singing the "Te Deum". They called their settlement El Parage de Yerba Buena—meaning "The Little Valley of the Good Herb"—after an aromatic vine found in the area (*Micromeria chamissonis* to the botanists). Not until 1847, under American rule, did it become known by the name the 16th-Century mariner Sebastian Cermeño had bestowed upon the stretch of barren coast 50 miles to the north.

The Franciscan friars established their mission a mile or two to the south of the Presidio; it would become known as the Mission Dolores—meaning "Mission of Sorrows"—after a small lake in the vicinity called Lagoon of Our Lady of Sorrows. The mission was built, we should remember, with the prime object of converting the local Indians to Christianity. Convert many of them the friars did—without, it appears, resorting to the brutality we have since tended to associate with that process throughout the Spanish Empire. By 1800, some 30,000 Indians had accepted the Catholic faith handed down to them by the friars of San Francisco and the three other missions that had been set up in the Bay area. For more than 30 years after that, the fathers who manned these four Catholic outposts had almost unlimited authority over the lives of the Indians who submitted to their influence. But in 1833 the mission lands throughout California were secularized by the government of Mexico (which had become independent of Spain in 1821), with the result that the Bay area missions became no more than parish churches for the communities around them. They remain intact and much-visited today—the most enduring testimony to the Spanish culture that once dominated this land.

Nearly half the people who live in the Mission District of San Francisco nowadays are of Hispanic background, though Catholicism no longer has the streets to itself. Just across the road from the Mission Dolores, beyond a belt of palm trees, is St. Matthew's Lutheran Church. Around the corner is the evangelical Lighthouse Full Gospel. And on the edge of the next block is a funeral home whose business is conducted on behalf of all denominations.

The mission itself is now identified as Californian Registered Historical Landmark Number 784. But it is still a living church as well, and a visitor cannot help but be moved by its spirit. In a part of the world where life-styles have changed more often and more radically than anywhere else, this tiny outpost of imperial Spain has not only survived, it has remained essentially the same, faithful to its old ways and deeply impressive for that. The pink-tiled roof juts deeply over white adobe walls four feet thick, made by the local Indians. The few small windows high up on those walls are glazed yellow to filter the sun, because the missionaries from the south were used to hot and glaring summers. Attached to the mission is a small museum where you can inspect some of the wooden pegs and hand-wrought nails that went into the building of the church. A breviary is there, too, its leather back scuffed and its metal clasps tarnished with age: it belonged to Padre Palou, the first priest in charge.

But the spirit of those times is most palpable within the mission itself. It drifts down like a blessing from the low, wood-beamed roof of the chancel and nave, which the Indians, using vegetable dyes, stained the colours of rust, grey and magnolia. It is in the fragrance of candle wax that floats within those white adobe walls. And its essence is captured on a tympanum above the font, where two Indians are represented offering a child to a Franciscan friar for baptism.

Faith may have been strong in this little community, but the garrison in the Presidio was not. When the English explorer Captain Frederick Beechey sailed into the bay in 1826, his professional eye was startled by the neglect of the military there; the fortifications apparently consisted of three rusty cannon and little else, and the troops were generally beholden to the mission priests for their food. The resources of Mexico were too stretched to maintain proper defences so far to the north. Yet, from the beginning of Mexican rule, it had been clear that military action would sooner or later be required if the Bay area was to remain in Mexican hands. The acquisitive gleam was in several eyes early in the 19th Century. President Andrew Jackson wanted an American footing in California. The British Hudson's Bay Company, whose trappers had spoken well of the area, was showing interest. And a hundred miles north of Yerba Buena, the Russians had a base from which they pursued the seal and the sea otter

A Sunny Citizenry

For countless Americans and migrants from every part of the world, San Francisco has always had a special mystique born of its charming setting and pleasant climate. In the mid-19th Century, dreams of easy fortune lured to the city the prospectors of the great California Gold Rush and today dreams still inspire a multitude of others to settle around the Bay in the hope of finding an El Dorado of the spirit. Of course, many high hopes are frustrated, but the smiling faces you so often notice in the streets suggest that, for a great many people, the quest for felicity has been fulfilled.

wherever they could find these creatures—including the waters of the Bay.

The first non-Spaniard had come to town in 1822. An Englishman who deserted from a whaling ship, he converted to Catholicism, since only a Catholic had the right to own land. Soon, other newcomers began to arrive by sea. Most were New Englanders, drawn by the possibilities of commerce, and bringing with them the stern puritanical values and toughness that had been triumphantly tested against the British in the states bordering the Atlantic. Not that everyone who arrived in those early years was a man of unimpeachable steadiness. The Rocky Mountain fur trappers who filtered into California in search of beaver were the image of carefree independence. And one Eastern businessman, Jacob P. Leese, who came to town in 1836, exhibited a flamboyance that was later to be commonplace in the city. He sailed into the Bay with merchandise worth $12,000, enough timber to build himself a very large house, and an orchestra of six musicians; to celebrate the anniversary of the American Declaration of Independence on Leese's first Fourth of July in Yerba Buena, they played at a party that lasted two days and a night.

The combination of a nearly impotent garrison and strong American sympathies among the population made San Francisco an easy target when war broke out between the U.S. and Mexico in 1846. (One of the causes was an offer by the U.S. to purchase all of California for $25 million—interpreted by Mexico as further proof of the American territorial avarice that had recently been demonstrated by the annexation of Texas.) On July 9, 1846, the *USS Portsmouth* sailed into the Bay and disembarked sailors and marines without meeting any opposition. Once ashore, they unfurled the American flag and Captain John B. Montgomery took possession of California in the name of the United States. He was not annexing a large settlement by the Bay; the population was no more than a thousand or so—and it soon declined steeply. Most of the Mexicans fled south, and by 1847 only 459 civilians were left in San Francisco.

At the beginning of 1848, a tide turned in the city's fortunes. Gold was discovered about a hundred miles inland and San Francisco was swiftly overwhelmed by a flood of humanity, the likes of which the world may not have seen before or since. As they poured into the Bay in overladen ships and hurried on to the goldfields, they left a mark on the city as indelible as the increase in the number of its streets and the extension of its boundaries. These men—unlike the devout Spanish and Mexican settlers or most of the New England businessmen who preceded them— were dreamers *in excelsis*, wild with lust for sudden wealth. They lived on hope more than achievement, for the number who became rich was small —and this may have been their most lasting contribution to San Francisco. It set an example for others after them to keep going on hope, at times when all the facts seemed to call for despair.

At dawn, only an antiquated cannon occupies the damp courtyard of Fort Point, tucked beneath a landward arch of the Golden Gate Bridge. The fort, nowadays open to the public, was built in 1861 for coastal defence. It stands on the site of the 18th-Century Spanish Presidio, or military garrison, the first European settlement to be established on the Bay.

The rebuilding of the city after the appalling earthquake of 1906 is the most notable example of this trait, but the habit had been well-established long before then: earthquakes had previously flattened parts of the city in 1865 and again in 1868. Nor has the habit been confined to coping with earth tremors. In its early years, this city was constantly exposed to trial by flames as well. Its rambling wooden buildings were wiped out by a fire on Christmas Eve in 1849 and by the summer of 1851 the same thing had happened on five other occasions.

So often has fire flickered across the history of San Francisco that fire engines and fire-fighters occupy a peculiarly nostalgic place in the affections of its citizenry today. I doubt if any other city has two memorials to its firemen—both built with funds from the estate of Lillie Coit. She was a wealthy and wilful San Franciscan who, as a girl of eight in 1851, had been saved from death in a fire by Engine Company Number Five; after that, she could be found wherever Company Number Five happened to be, and she later became an honorary member of the San Francisco Fire Department. One of the memorials, a sculpture of three bronze figures rescuing a fourth, still stands in Washington Square. The other, the 170-foot Coit Tower on Telegraph Hill, is one of the city's great landmarks; the observant will be intrigued to note that its concrete tip has been fashioned in the shape of a fire-hose nozzle.

So often had the ability to live on hope been called forth in the first century of the city's life that we may think San Francisco was the obvious choice in 1945 as a meeting place for the leaders of a world who had a vision of the future. When Churchill, Roosevelt and Stalin met at Yalta and decided that San Francisco was where the United Nations should gather in conference for the first time, political considerations were doubtless to the fore; but it would be nice to believe that the politicians were not indifferent to symbolism as well. Here, at any rate, the statesmen gathered for a full two months to hammer out the United Nations Charter. They met in the Opera House, where the violinist Yehudi Menuhin played Beethoven with the San Francisco Symphony Orchestra to soothe (if it couldn't inspire) those tired old men of the world. The war with Japan was not yet over, but no one who was young in those days can ever forget what a dream seemed to brighten the Western sky that spring. It began to fade almost at once, as the statesmen returned whence they had come. Within a few months an atom bomb had been dropped on Hiroshima and Stalin had begun to swallow Eastern Europe.

But San Francisco continued to foster more than its share of dreamers. Not all of them have had a clear vision of their future. In the 1960s, the students of the University of California at Berkeley thought they saw a new way ahead and they used every available podium or publication to offer prescriptions for brotherly love and fair shares for all. Their Free Speech Movement had begun as a rebellion against an edict of the

Beneath leaden storm clouds, a row of palm trees lends a tropical air to Dolores Street, which runs through the city's mainly Spanish-speaking Mission District.

university authorities prohibiting all forms of political activity on the campus during the 1964 presidential election campaign. Eventually it grew into a massive student insurrection inflamed by a whole range of issues, including civil rights and the war in Vietnam. Campus demonstrations became the order of the day, as did bombardment by tear gas when the police attempted to bring the students to heel. This was a time when Negroes suddenly became blacks, when God was said to be dead and when women declared themselves alive as never before.

Uncomfortable as these transformations may have been for some of us —not the ideas they embodied but the violence with which they were sometimes proclaimed—it is as well to bear in mind that they were part of somebody's glorious dream. Revolution always is; and the Berkeley discontents expressed a hunger for revolution. So too, in its own untidy way, did the Beat Generation in the 1950s and its transformation into the Hippie scene later on, with all the turning-on, tuning-in and dropping-out that subsequently enlivened and occasionally disfigured this city.

I see that I have flitted over too much history too quickly in tracing the blithe spirit that seems to have consistently carried San Francisco forward. We will take it more slowly from now on. But let us forget history for the moment and wonder why it is that San Francisco remains such an attraction. It is a curiosity of the place that scarcely any of one's friends and acquaintances there have been born and bred in San Francisco. The city is not, of course, exceptional in this characteristic: the same could probably be said of many major cities in the world. New York is certainly full of Americans from every state in the Union, drawn to Manhattan by professional ambition or plain economic opportunity. I myself was propelled towards London from Lancashire many years ago by the same urge to pursue my trade where it seemed to offer me the greatest rewards of every kind.

The very strange, and possibly unique, feature of San Francisco is that people still migrate there in some quantity without the incentives that exist in either New York or London. Employers in San Francisco tend to pay lower wages than they would have to in many other large American cities—the reason being that people are eager to live there at almost any price. In New York, salaries for comparable jobs are often 20 or even 25 per cent higher. There is said to be a small army of Berkeley graduates with doctorates who wash dishes in restaurants and accept other manual labour because local teaching posts are hard to come by and they prefer to live on the Bay rather than use their qualifications in some other part of the country. The unemployment figures for San Francisco are invariably a notch or two higher than the average for the United States. Yet people still crave to be here. What on earth pulls them all in?

It may seem ludicrously trivial to suggest that, partly at least, the weather has something to do with it. San Francisco's climate is not as sunny as that

An outfielder on the San Francisco Giants baseball team (left) makes a running catch during a game with the visiting Cincinnati Reds. Originally based in New York, the Giants moved to San Francisco in 1958. The team's new home stadium at Candlestick Park (right) was built in 1960 with public funds and accommodates crowds of up to 60,000. It stands at an edge of the Bay and is known as the windiest baseball stadium in the U.S.

enjoyed in other parts of California, but it is generally mellow, not given to extremes. Winters are mild, with an average January temperature of 50°F —although it can pour like a monsoon then, in great gusts of rain that flood roads, cause trees to topple and start landslides on some of those 43 hills. Summers never become really hot, as they do further inland; in September, the warmest month, the mean temperature is 61.5°F.

Summer is much more celebrated for its fogs, which creep in from the Pacific, drawn from the cool of the ocean by hot air rising inland from the valleys of the Sierra Nevada and the fiery Nevada desert. In a finger at first, then in a bank, the fog comes through the Golden Gate, toying for a while with the Golden Gate Bridge and making it, in that time, un-questionably the most beautiful bridge in the world. Foghorns begin to sound. There are about 30 of these, strategically placed on bridges, buoys and cliffs around the Bay—soprano, bass and baritone, with a handful whose signals resemble the moans of a rather sick cow. In 1954, a lecturer at Berkeley, William S. Hart, was so moved by them that he composed a foghorn concerto, performed with tapes he had made around the Bay. ("The burden of the music," wrote the *San Francisco Chronicle's* critic, "is carried by the piano, which dances along in splashing, melodious style, playing around the foghorn notes, incorporating them into its own musical fabric.") A European is apt to regard fog as some sort of plague. But San Franciscans speak of their fog affectionately, as something they would not be without, that peps them up when they were beginning to feel too sleepy in the summer sun; and they make mild jests at the ex-pense of tourists who have come to the city clad for maximum sun-tan, but who wander around in the fog getting goose pimples instead.

Although the evenness of the climate gives the city a decided advantage over most places on earth, it cannot entirely explain the magnetism of San Francisco, any more than a beautiful setting and a generally beguiling

appearance can. But if an easy-going social climate is added to these other traits, then the inducements begin to seem sufficient. This is not to say that San Francisco's society is free from stresses and strains. It would be foolish to believe that the city represents perfection for every one of its people, as some of its dafter publicists would have outsiders think. (In the area covered by the San Francisco Police Department—45 square miles, with some 715,000 inhabitants—an average of three murders are committed every week, and the record of lesser crimes is worse than in most other American cities.) But San Francisco possesses an attitude of tolerance that is often missing elsewhere. More than in most cities, you can be what you like here and behave as you will, so long as you do not impose yourself on other people.

No one who visits San Francisco for the first time can fail to be aware of the pleasantly relaxed atmosphere. You are not perpetually admonished by well-wishers about the dangers of getting mugged, as visitors usually are in New York. It seems true that shop assistants here are more amiable than elsewhere, less bent on treating their customers as components of the cash register; when they say "Have a nice day", they sound as though they mean it and not as if it were a ritual phrase learned to help trade. Watch people move about the streets if you want to appreciate what San Francisco has done to them. Except at rush hour, they tend to stroll. There is nothing comparable here to downtown New York or the heart of London, where the word "perambulation" may now be considered redundant except at weekends, having long since been banished by the general push and shove.

Many of San Francisco's secrets as "a place to get to if you can" were contained in Jack Kerouac's classic novel *On the Road*, which conveyed the feeling of the Beat Generation more perfectly, I am assured, than anything else ever written. The main characters are two restless souls named Sal Paradise and Dean Moriarty, and much of the plot concerns a trip across America to the West Coast.

At the beginning of the novel, when Sal Paradise is in New York and scheming to meet up with Dean and begin their carefree journey to the Pacific, he has a very incomplete idea of what awaits him. Still, he senses that something desirable lies there and that, at the end of the experience, he will find what it is. "Somewhere along the line I knew there'd be girls, visions, everything; somewhere along the line the pearl would be handed to me." Much later, after his arrival in San Francisco, he fetches up in a bar in The Fillmore, the district where most of the city's blacks live, and watches a singer named Connie Jordan splashing his sweat into the audience and kicking over the microphone in the frenzy of his act. "I never saw such crazy musicians," says Sal. "Everybody in Frisco blew. It was the end of the continent; they didn't give a damn."

Those two quotations, I dare say, would strike a note of recognition in

Judah Street, on San Francisco's west side, appears to plunge headlong into the Pacific as it undulates down from the vicinity of Sunset Heights, one of the city's 43 hills. The tracks and overhead power lines are used by modern electric streetcars which, along with the ancient and much-loved cable cars of the downtown districts, keep alive the city's century-old tradition of street railways.

many a migrant to San Francisco who has never identified closely with the Beats, the Hippies or any of the other footloose clan who, in their time, have seen Sal Paradise as a household god. "Somewhere along the line the pearl would be handed to me" is not far distant from the philosophy that brought the Gold-Rushers to town; and a memory of those days may have persuaded many a respectable fellow with a wife and two kids that here was where his kind of opportunity knocked. As for the freedom sought at the end of the continent, that idea is embedded in the American unconscious. Americans have been moving west, in search of freedom, almost from the day the Pilgrim Fathers landed on the New England shore. Perhaps inevitably, California has become the most populous state in the nation, even though it is not the biggest.

Some of the west-moving migrants have been driven as much as drawn, concluding that if they couldn't make it elsewhere, they might make it in California. Depressingly, a number of them haven't made it in this last refuge either and the golden dream has turned into a dark night of the soul. This is especially true of San Francisco. The most miserable thing about the city is its suicide rate, which is about four times the national average and almost twice that of California as a whole.

Yet a community consisting largely of immigrants is bound to have more than its fair share of vitality and resilience. San Francisco certainly has a very youthful air—which is nothing less than a geriatric triumph, since a third of the population is more than 60 years old. Perhaps a bit uneasy with its own sappy atmosphere, the city can sometimes be caught trying to speed up its history, to give itself the eminence of age. The City Lights Bookshop on Columbus Avenue, which was a headquarters for the Beat Generation and remains a touchstone to its legatees, makes a point of announcing that it has been "A Literary Meeting Place since 1953" —to which the only fitting response seems to be "Wow!" But such tendencies run counter to San Francisco's genuine stripling spirit.

Men wearing collars, ties and suits are few and far between in San Francisco, except on weekdays in the heart of the business district; and even there, dress is liable to be much more casual than is the norm among businessmen throughout the world. The matrons of San Francisco do not often have to resort to those techniques of camouflage designed to keep onlookers guessing about their real age; more than most, they are able to rely upon their liveliness to see them through. The last time I was there, a survivor of the 1906 earthquake was still around, a lady of 90-odd who didn't look much over 70 and who was still capable of flirting gallantly with a man half a century younger.

Youth has the awful drawback of being resented by the old unless the old are very wise and balanced, and I suspect that the youthful soul of San Francisco is rather deeply resented by some older cities that should know better. I cannot think of any other reason (unless it be self-obsession) why New York should be so disdainful of this place; New Yorkers invariably imply that San Francisco is pretty and nice to visit, but not really very important. San Francisco bears these snubs equably, however, and gets on with her own business. If she feels threatened by anybody, it is mostly by Oakland across the Bay—a rather shabby place by comparison, but increasingly superseding the port of San Francisco as a centre of international commerce.

The rivalry between the two cities is by no means new, and San Franciscans have long reserved their sharpest comments for these neighbours over the water. When San Francisco was damaged by the earthquake of 1865, from which Oakland emerged unscathed, the writer Bret Harte caustically remarked that there were some things the earth could not swallow. And when the completion of the Bay Area Rapid Transit system (universally known as BART) in 1974 at last enabled people here to travel by underground train, San Franciscans joked that the whole scheme had been devised so that they could get over to Oakland—only, of course, if they absolutely had to—without anyone noticing.

These wisecracks tell another truth about San Francisco. I have known affectionate citizens to call her Baghdad-by-the-Bay, in an attempt to capture her exotic charms; but if she is to be likened to any other place on earth, then I think it should be to Venice—a city that at the height of her splendour boastfully styled herself the Serenissima, the Most Serene. Both have much beauty, both are girt about by water, and both have pasts that were dark and brilliant by turns. Both also live under the threat of natural disaster. Sal Paradise summed it up well. When he had made his crazy way to this end of the continent, he saw "stretched out ahead of us the fabulous white city of San Francisco . . . with the blue Pacific and its advancing wall of potato-patch fog beyond, and smoke and goldenness in the late afternoon of time". Truly, another Serenissima had been found.

Riddles for the Eye

Steps meet California Street at a disconcerting angle where a woman descends from the A. P. Giannini Plaza, named after the founder of the Bank of America.

Confined on its narrow, hilly peninsula, San Francisco presents unusual problems to planners and architects, whose often ingenious solutions give the City by the Bay much of its eye-catching appeal. Like other American cities, San Francisco has for the most part adopted a grid pattern of streets which, superimposed on the uneven terrain, creates steep slopes, sharp crests and sudden descents, so that driving a car is like taking a roller-coaster ride and simply walking can become a minor feat of mountaineering. As a local wit once put it: "When you get tired of walking around San Francisco, you can always lean against it." The designers and engineers seem to have been strongly influenced by nature's virtuosity—creating buildings with sloping walls, tunnelling straight through hills, revelling in banks of soaring steps and weirdly juxtaposed planes.

A battered car is parked on a hill with wheels to the kerb, as required by law.

Cresting the brow of Divisadero Street, a driver prepares to test both brakes and nerves in a precipitous descent towards the waterfront district of Marina.

The Qantas building in Union Square rises behind the pigeon-bedecked base of the Naval Monument, which marks an 1898 victory in the Spanish-American War.

A view through the Stockton Street Tunnel, which links downtown San Francisco with North Beach, gives the illusion that the sky has dropped below street level.

A man on the terraced slope of Alta Plaza park appears to be waist high in steps. The stairway is a copy of the one outside the famous casino at Monte Carlo.

A guest is dwarfed amid the stepped tiers of balconies on the angled north face of the Hyatt Regency Hotel, built in 1973 and renowned for its innovative design.

Almost lost among the streetside hydrangeas, cars wind their way down the eight switchbacks of Lombard Street, known as the crookedest street in the world.

2

Money, Money, Money

As you drive along the Bayshore Freeway north into San Francisco from the airport, your *eye* cannot escape a prominent sign on the slope of a hill. Someone has whitewashed a heap of stones up there to spell out to all comers the fact that they are passing through "South San Francisco Industrial City". South San Francisco happens to be a distinct municipality, not even located in the same county as its namesake; and the hillside boast is a sad reminder of the dispersal of the Serenissima's own manufacturing activities. During the 19th Century, San Francisco proper was the chief industrial centre of the West, but since before the First World War it has been steadily losing ground—much of it to other cities scattered around the Bay.

The most notable example of this outward drift is the local canning industry, which keeps almost an entire continent supplied with fruit and vegetables from the fertile soils of California. Originally set up in the 1850s and 1860s in downtown San Francisco, it was driven by its own success to expansion in spacious Oakland. There, across the Bay, it flourished even more, eventually becoming the region's largest single industry—and, as a by-product providing a job for Jack London until he lit out for distant parts of the world in search of more stimulating plots for his novels and short stories.

If the Bay area can be said to have an industrial capital, then, it is Oakland—but industry sprawls almost from top to bottom of the inland sea's eastern shore. Standard Oil has refineries over there; General Motors, Ford and Chrysler assemble automobiles there; Kaiser Steel and United States Steel have forges and foundries there; many other big names in American industry are located there. Of the nation's 100 largest manufacturing concerns, almost half are represented in plants and warehouses and other facilities ranged across the water from the city that started it all. And on the south-western shore of the Bay, in a 10-by-25-mile area formally known as Santa Clara County but often called Silicon Valley, scores more companies turn out high-technology items: silicon chips for computer circuitry and a welter of other miniature marvels of the electronic age.

San Francisco can only muster peanuts by comparison. Nowadays, a naval repair yard occupies Hunter's Point, just opposite Oakland, and Bethlehem Steel has foundries on land nearby. Further down the San Francisco side of the Bay but still within the city limits are some railroad repair shops, some cement and gravel plants, a sugar refinery, and one

Hurrying from a subway station on the sleek Bay Area Rapid Transit system, known by the acronym BART, an executive heads for his office in the financial district. San Francisco has been the financial centre of the American West ever since the days of the Gold Rush, and its banking activities today rank second only to New York in the United States as a whole.

In the half-light of early morning, an employee of the Pacific Coast Stock Exchange on Sansome Street arrives for work (left). He must be at his desk by 7 a.m. because the exchange opens at the same time as Wall Street, and New York is three hours ahead of San Francisco. Seated at computer consoles on the floor of the exchange, brokers (right)—together with colleagues at the exchange branch in Los Angeles—frequently conclude share-transactions worth more than $30 million by the close of a day's business.

or two other bits and pieces. They do not, by any stretch of the imagination, add up to an industrial city. Fewer people work in factories here than in offices. The biggest single segment of the work-force is to be found among the service industries, running the restaurants, hotels and other establishments that draw a good part of their patronage from a thriving tourist trade. The next largest group are the labourers in wholesale trade; and after them come the toilers in finance, insurance and real estate. The most significant thing about San Francisco as a source of bread and butter is that its proportion of white-collar workers, at just over 60 per cent of the working population, exceeds that of any other large city of the United States.

You could almost guess as much after once observing rush hour in the city centre. Stand on Market Street around 9 a.m. and you will see San Franciscans breaking into a gait that verges on jogging. As they pour off the cable cars and the electrified buses, as they blink into the daylight from the underground rapid-transit stations, they quite transform the normally easy-going pace of that gracious thoroughfare. They come in such numbers that, for a period of one hour or so, they obscure the stylish brick sidewalks of Market Street.

Look carefully at this throng hurrying to work: these are the rising young executives and the secretaries of the town—the citizens most closely concerned with how San Francisco pays her way—and there are a lot of them streaming, at this very moment, down the steepness of California Street aboard its cable cars, hanging on to the running-boards like so many clusters of grapes. From Market Street and California Street they proceed briskly in all directions through the city centre, into the skyscrapers and the lesser buildings, to tot up their figures and flick their

typewriters and make calculations with far-reaching effects. Many head for Montgomery Street, known near and far as the Wall Street of the West.

It is all very different from New York, however, in at least one obvious respect. You never feel, in downtown San Francisco, the claustrophobia that among the skyscrapers of Manhattan can so often depress the soul. San Francisco has relatively few really tall buildings of 30 storeys and more; but a great number do rise pretty high off the ground. Nevertheless, there are so many gaps between them occupied by lesser fry, that you are not constantly reduced to the proportions of a bug trying to make its way through the intricacies of an herbaceous border. Plenty of sky is always visible in one direction or another. And happily San Francisco is relatively free of New York's chronic building frenzy: the awful proliferation of construction sites where one building has just been demolished to make room for a more profitable successor.

Downtown San Francisco went through a radical development phase in the late 1960s and early 1970s but (to the relief of most citizens) seems to have settled down to more orderly growth. The most arresting monument to the downtown rearrangements has been the pyramid built in 1972 as the headquarters of the Transamerica Corporation—a colossal holding company with interests in ventures ranging from insurance to movie-making; set on a network of concrete stilts, the building rises through 48 floors of financial wizardry, to a gleaming white pinnacle that is visible from almost any point in the city. An entire block of 19th-Century structures was razed to make room for this new landmark, a circumstance guaranteed to perturb the many San Franciscans who find no virtue in modernization. On the site chosen for the pyramid stood the only downtown buildings that had survived undamaged after the fire that swept across San Francisco in the wake of the 1906 earthquake. Soldiers had been prepared to blow them up to make a firebreak against the spreading inferno but, in the name of civic pride, were urged to tackle more difficult alternatives, since the buildings already had a noteworthy past: one had been the home of the city's first law library; others served as studios for early artists and writers.

Close by the Transamerica pyramid, at the corner of Sansome and Vine, stands the Stock Exchange, whose members are among the earliest risers in town; they have to be on the floor by 7 o'clock every morning, to coincide with the opening of Wall Street, which is not only 3,000 miles away but an inconvenient three hours ahead as well. There are a number of ways in which San Francisco must play second fiddle to New York, and this is but one of them. Also, increasingly in recent years, the city's stockbroking trade has been taking a back seat to Los Angeles, whose metropolitan population exceeds that of the Bay area by some three million. This situation has produced pressure from the south to consolidate the two operations of the Pacific Stock Exchange and locate it in Los

Metamorphosis of a Mission Town

1542 Portuguese mariner Juan Rodriguez Cabrillo makes first exploration of the California coast, but fails to discover entrance to San Francisco Bay

1579 English navigator Francis Drake anchors north of the Golden Gate at inlet now known as Drake's Bay; he calls the land New Albion and claims it for Elizabeth I of England

1595 Shipwrecked captain Sebastian Cermeño annexes same stretch of indented coastline for Spain and names it Puerto de San Francisco

1769 San Francisco Bay first seen by a European: Sergeant José de Ortega, a scout on Spanish overland expedition under leadership of Don Gaspar de Portolá

1772 Spanish party led by its priest, Father Juan Crespi, and Lieutenant Pedro Fages skirt the eastern shore of Bay in search of site for new Franciscan mission

1776 Captain Juan Bautista de Anza chooses locations for future Presidio, or military post, and mission of San Francisco. First party of 244 settlers from Mexico, headed by Lieutenant José Moraga, arrives at the Bay. Settlement is named El Parage de Yerba Buena (The Little Valley of the Good Herb) after a sweet-smelling shrub found growing there

1821 Mexico wins independence from Spain

1824 California formally becomes a province of new Republic of Mexico

1841 British fur-trading firm, Hudson's Bay Company, establishes an agency in Yerba Buena

1844 First American to settle in Yerba Buena, William Hinckley, elected mayor

1846 War breaks out between Mexico and the U.S. Captain John Montgomery enters Bay on "USS Portsmouth"; in town plaza, he announces U.S. annexation of California. Entrance to Bay is christened the Golden Gate ("Chrysopylae") by U.S. army captain John C. Frémont

1847 Yerba Buena, with population of 1,000, officially renamed San Francisco. First newspaper, "The California Star", appears

1848 Gold discovered by Scottish-born carpenter, James Marshall, at John Sutter's sawmill on the American River in foothills of the Sierra Nevada. Treaty of Guadalupe Hidalgo ends Mexican-American War, ceding California to the United States

1849 First Gold-Rush steamer, "California" arrives from New York, inaugurating regular steamboat service between East and West. Thousands of gold seekers, nicknamed "forty-niners", pour into San Francisco. City suffers first of six major fires that strike in period of 18 months

1850 Semaphore station built on Telegraph Hill to signal approach of vessels. Levi Strauss, a Bavarian immigrant, begins his business of supplying reinforced canvas pants to goldminers. Population of San Francisco reaches 25,000

1851 First Committee of Vigilance organized to combat gangs of hoodlums

1852 Wells Fargo & Company founded to transport mail by ship and stagecoach between San Francisco and New York. Chinese population swells to 18,000

1856 Second Committee of Vigilance organized

1859 Discovery of fabulous silver deposits in the Sierra Nevada, just beyond California's eastern border, pours new wealth into San Francisco, now financial centre of the West

1861 Outbreak of American Civil War; majority of San Franciscans support Union (anti-slavery) cause. Direct telegraphic links opened between San Francisco and the East. Fort Point completed to bolster city's defences in event of Confederate attack

1864 Mark Twain settles in San Francisco, where he works as staff reporter for the "Morning Call" newspaper and begins writing stories and vignettes of the city's life

1869 Central Pacific and Union Pacific railroad lines joined at Promontory, Utah, completing first transcontinental rail route. Some 15,000 Chinese labourers contribute to construction

Angeles, instead of having floors working simultaneously in both cities. When a vote of all exchange members was taken early in 1978, only 44 per cent could be mustered in support of San Francisco's resistance to the idea, and its exchange operations would now be dead or moribund if the proposal had not required a two-thirds majority for passage. Many people think that the city's Stock Exchange building, with its vaguely classical front and its Diego Rivera frescoes inside, is bound to tumble to Progress sooner or later.

No such worries attend the banking business of San Francisco, though it, too, is ever-conscious of New York, which has always been the central money market of the United States as well as the leader in foreign exchange markets. But San Francisco bankers hope to develop a foreign exchange market on their own account, pinning these ambitions on San Francisco's strategic position opposite the rising nations of South-East Asia and, above all, on the continuing financial growth of Japan. They speak in glowing terms of the Pacific Basin's potential, estimating conservatively that its wealth should grow at a rate of 5 or 6 per cent annually. According to the local financiers, Japanese banks will increasingly be unable to handle all the loans and investments that need to be made on their side of the Pacific, and the Californians believe they can do business there on a mounting scale. Such long-range thinking helps explain how San Francisco has maintained its status as the biggest banking centre in the American West.

Banking acumen at its sharpest has been responsible for the steady ascent of the Bank of America, whose 52-storey building at Montgomery, Pine, Kearny and California Streets ranks as the tallest in town. Built in 1969, that marble-and-glass pillar is, in fact, the command post of a banking empire larger than any other in the world. To say this is a bit like pointing to a gap in the clouds and announcing solemnly that there lies the philosophical centre of the universe; one expects a reaction of blank boredom or a mindless yell of "Eureka". But it means that the gentlemen controlling the Bank of America can lay their hands on more money, if pushed to it, than any other bank on earth—in excess of $80 billion. Acquiring such financial resources would be an impressive achievement no matter where it happened, but it seems to me particularly so in the United States, whose laws forbid a bank to open a branch anywhere in the country outside its state of origin.

How the Bank of America attained its present position is essentially the tale of one man's genius and energy. If you want the archetypal American success story, then consider Amadeo Peter Giannini's rise to power. He was born in 1870, the son of a modest hotel-keeper who had migrated from Italy to the town of San Jose, at the southern tip of the Bay. For a time, young Giannini worked in the fruit-and-vegetable wholesale trade and trafficked in real estate on the side. Then, in 1902, he moved into banking as a director of San Francisco's Columbus Savings and Loan Society, a small institution patronized by the Italian community of North Beach. Two years later, after a row with his fellow directors, he opened an establishment of his own, the Bank of Italy. He started out with three employees and $150,000 in capital. On the first day he accepted 28 deposits amounting to at least $8,000—and never looked back.

His next big step forward was the result of the 1906 earthquake. With most of downtown San Francisco afire and the flames fast approaching his bank, Giannini obtained a wagon and horses with which to remove his cash and records to safety, though he had to leave behind his new Burroughs adding machine, whose $375 cost had recently strained his resources. The larger banks in the city left their valuables in the protection of big vaults, which Giannini did not possess; but it took them some time after the fire to get at the safes buried in the ruins (the steel doors were untouchably hot for many days) and so, long before his more powerful rivals were back in full working order, Giannini had started business again with a bag of money beside a plank counter he set up on the city's water-front. This feat created such confidence in his bank that, before the year was out, he had doubled his business.

His Midas touch never deserted him. Within a few years he was opening branches throughout the state; by the 1920s the Bank of Italy was California's chief backer of agriculture, holding mortgages on 12,000 farms. By 1930, Giannini's creation—wearing the new name of the Bank of America—had become the fourth largest bank in the United States;

In an idealized view of a goldfield painted in 1850, a year after the start of the great California Gold Rush, two prospecting miners shovel gold-bearing soil into a sluice and break up the heavier clods. Another man downstream, kneeling in front of a larger sifting device, pans in the ice-cold mountain water for loose gold flakes or nuggets.

and the next year it opened its first foreign branch, in London. The crowning moment of Giannini's life arrived in 1945, when the Bank of America passed the Chase National of New York and became the largest bank in the world. By the time he died in 1949, he left behind an institution with resources worth $8.2 billion.

In the eyes of knowledgeable financiers, Giannini's greatness in the field of modern banking is equalled, or perhaps surpassed, only by J. P. Morgan. But Morgan accumulated his wealth almost entirely by doing business with the wealthy and with combinations of the wealthy. Giannini did not disdain them—and big business in California since his death has been much enlarged by Bank of America money—but at the same time he never strayed from his origins among those with small savings. The Bank of America empire is based on piecemeal deposits made week by week at more than a thousand branches throughout California.

To anyone who has ever enjoyed a good Western movie, the most familiar banking name in San Francisco is not Giannini's prodigy but the establishment of Wells Fargo & Company. This firm was founded in San Francisco in 1852 by Henry Wells and William G. Fargo, who had already made fortunes back East by building up an express company that delivered gold, lightweight valuables and mail (in its mail-carrying role, the company was efficient and its fees so low that the U.S. Post Office had to cut its own rates to avoid losing business). Out West, Wells Fargo & Company grew into a corporate giant: it opened branch offices in scores of towns across the frontier, offered a wide range of banking services, and developed an unmatched network of stagecoach routes. Today, with a fine sense of history, this firm has preserved at its Montgomery Street headquarters a stagecoach that it used to operate between Hangtown, near Coloma in California, and Carson City in Nevada, along with the stern injunctions that passengers were expected to observe: "In cold weather don't ride with tight-fitting boots, shoes or gloves. When the driver asks you to get off and walk do so without grumbling, he won't request it unless absolutely necessary. If the team runs away—sit still and take your chances. If you jump, nine times out of ten you will get hurt."

Under a glass case near the stagecoach the proprietors have arranged a show of the gold ore that put Wells Fargo—like San Francisco itself— well and truly on its feet. Here, in a variety of colours and consistencies, are flakes from a dozen different sites in the Sierra Nevada foothills, and little heaps of dust that were panned out of riverbeds. One display missing at Wells Fargo is the very first nugget of all, the nickel-sized piece that started the California Gold Rush: the Bancroft Library at Berkeley has pre-empted it, along with Francis Drake's brass plate.

This nugget was found on January 24, 1848, in the tailrace of a saw-mill at Coloma, 100 miles or so inland amid the gentle hills that roll up

to the High Sierra. The discovery was made by James Marshall, a 35-year-old carpenter, who had come West from New Jersey by way of Oregon and was hired by John Sutter, the leading landowner in the area, to build the Coloma mill. "He was," Sutter recalled much later in life, "a very curious man, quarrelled with nearly everybody, though I could get along with him very well. He was a spiritualist. He used to dress in buckskin and wear a serape. I thought him half crazy."

A photograph of Marshall reveals a face that might have belonged to a New England schoonerman of the period, or a certain kind of eternal Scot; it is very severe, brooding over things that are not of this world. Since the picture was taken years after Marshall's momentous find, his appearance is scarcely surprising, for his life became a tragedy from 1848 on. The claims he and Sutter made to gold found on the Coloma property were disregarded, and Marshall himself had no further success as a miner. He was harassed by other miners, who ridiculed his notions of supernatural power and threatened to lynch him if he didn't lead them to more treasure. He became a man with a grudge against life, and his bitterness was intensified when the state of California reluctantly gave him a pension of $200 a year as the discoverer of gold, and then cut off the pension four years later. He spent his last years working as a blacksmith and selling his autograph for pennies.

There wasn't much to San Francisco in the winter of 1848. It had only just ceased to be Yerba Buena, a place "with no commerce, no wealth, no power, and without a name, save as a small trading post and mission station", as a visitor recorded the year before. It had a mayor, it had one

In a photograph taken at the height of the California Gold Rush, probably in late 1850, the masts of at least 500 sailing ships tower above the San Francisco waterfront. The vessels had been hired to bring fortune hunters from all over the world, but when their crews joined the headlong scramble for the goldfields, they were abandoned and left to rot at anchor.

The "Apollo", one of several deserted ships that were converted into warehouses, offers services to traders, shoppers and sightseers. The text accompanying this lithograph advertised all kinds of merchandise for sale, as well as a storage space for trunks. Although the owners claimed the premises to be safe from fire, the converted ship burned in 1851.

street, and it had a newspaper; not much else. The newspaper, the *California Star*, was owned by Sam Brannan, a Mormon, who had sailed through the Golden Gate a few weeks after the American annexation of 1846, leading a shipload of fellow believers to found a new colony in California on the instructions of Brigham Young. Brannan was a bull of a man, whether engaged in preaching, campaigning for public education, organizing the first jury trial in California or arranging his own future in the property market. He occupied the opposite end of the human spectrum from James Marshall.

Brannan himself had taken off for Coloma in the autumn of 1847, to open a store on Sutter's property and he was up there when Marshall discovered gold. Later, he rushed through the streets of San Francisco with the electrifying news and an old quinine bottle containing gold dust to prove it. The town had 900 inhabitants that day and only seven were left behind a few hours later. The rest were struggling towards the bush-clad hills of El Dorado, with the chief apostle, Brannan, at their head.

Soon the horde was digging feverishly along the banks of the American River, from which the revealing tailrace flowed—and Brannan could be found striding around to collect what he was pleased to call "the Lord's tithe" on their takings. When, subsequently, Brigham Young despatched a message from Salt Lake City to claim this revenue for the Mormon cause, Sam Brannan sent back the envoy empty-handed. "You tell Brigham that I'll give up the Lord's money when he gives me a receipt signed by the Lord, and no sooner!"

It was Brannan's newspaper that told the world what was happening up there. On April 1, the *Star* produced a special edition of 2,000 copies, which was designed to promote Eastern interest in California generally and was carried inland towards the Mississippi Valley by mule train. That issue included an article by a physician, Dr. Victor Fourgeaud, entitled "Prospects of California"—a fond, discursive piece explaining that the future of this Pacific land was based on much more than potential mineral wealth. But in his article he wrote: "We saw a few days ago, a beautiful specimen of gold from the mine newly discovered on the American Fork. From all accounts the mine is immensely rich—and already, we learn, the gold from it, collected at random and without any trouble, has become an article of trade in the upper settlements. This precious metal abounds in this country." By August, the news had reached the other side of the continent and was republished in the *New York Herald*. From that moment, the Gold Rush was on with a vengeance.

Already, thousands of Californians were heading for the hills and word of the fabulous find was spreading down the Pacific coastline to incite others as far away as South America. In June and July alone, $250,000 worth of gold came from the diggings; this was paltry compared with what the hills were soon to yield, but it was enough to confirm Dr. Fourgeaud's gentle assumption. By New Year's Day, 1849, 6,000 miners were at work up at the diggings. San Francisco itself had blossomed with tents housing 2,000 new arrivals, most of whom stayed only long enough to get their land legs and organize themselves for the journey inland to the Sierra foothills.

A passenger on the first steamship to come through the Golden Gate said that all the canvas pitched hastily on the surrounding sandhills suggested a battleground rather than a village. He arrived at the end of February, 1849, aboard the sidewheeler *California*, which had sailed from New York the previous October. The ship had room for 210 passengers, but by the time it had rounded Cape Horn and steamed north as far as Panama, a thousand or more gold seekers were clamouring to get aboard. Some had set out from New Orleans and canoed across the isthmus to reach the port on the other side, where they could intercept the steamer when it stopped for fuel and supplies; others had struggled up to Panama from Peru and Chile, or down from Mexico. When the *California* eventually reached San Francisco, she was wallowing in the water, dangerously overloaded. She was at once deserted by both the passengers and crew, the first of many such ships that were to be abandoned for the pursuit of gold. By the autumn of 1849, the waters of the Bay had 600 empty ships riding at anchor, and the number was to increase as the 1850s drew on.

By then armadas were regularly setting out for California from the East Coast of America as gold fever became epidemic throughout the New England and New York states. Joining the ne'er-do-wells who had nothing to lose, farmers abandoned their farms, workmen their jobs; clerks quit their counting houses, preachers their pulpits. One-quarter of Nantucket Island's voting population went West in nine months; 800 men from the whaling port of New Bedford did likewise. Some of these "forty-niners" struggled overland across the continent, enduring great hardships *en route*. In a few cases, these adventurers attempted to travel in style: 50 young Bostonians in one group adopted grey-and-gold uniforms, took seven wagons, 31 mules, four horses, six dogs, two servants and four musicians, and finally made their destination after six months and great casualties among the mules. But the majority of the gold hunters travelled by sea, paying as much as $1,000 apiece for the passage around the Horn. Even a passage from Panama to San Francisco could cost between $200 and $600, depending on the comforts and extras they were prepared to buy. The money for these fares was often subscribed by companies of people who stayed at home on the understanding that they would receive a percentage of the fortunes that would be taken in the field.

To sustain this great new trade, there was a rapid growth in the East Coast shipbuilding industry. The Pacific Mail Steamship Company, owners of the *California*, built a new fleet of 29 vessels that took 175,000 people to San Francisco in the next decade. Between 1850 and 1854, Eastern yards launched 160 fast clipper ships to cope with the demand. Some vessels never completed that 15,000-mile voyage to the goldfields; in just two years, between 1851 and 1853, eleven steamers went down on the journey around Cape Horn. Thousands of passengers succumbed to disease *en route*.

For the survivors, the journey usually meant six months of misery. When heavily laden vessels sailed through stormy seas, their captains habitually jettisoned the passengers' baggage to improve the chances of staying afloat. Provisioning was often inadequate and hungry voyagers sometimes tried to make meals of the flying fish that skimmed aboard in the tropics. Water was frequently in such short supply that people thanked God for downpours that enabled them to catch rain in canvas sheets. Sea-sickness, scurvy and chilblains were a constant penance, even if nothing worse befell. The wonder is that they ever managed to keep up their spirits at all in conditions that were much worse than those of the two-week trans-Atlantic crossings of European migrants. But keep them up they did, croaking out the songs of adventure they brought with them to the goldfields of California. When the barque *Eliza* set sail from Massachusetts late in 1848, one of the passengers began singing (to the popular tune "Oh, Susannah!") these words:

> *I came from Salem City,*
> *With my washbowl on my knee,*
> *I'm going to California,*
> *The gold dust for to see.*

It rained all night the day I left,
The weather it was dry,
The sun so hot I froze to death,
Oh! brothers don't you cry.
Chorus: Oh! California,
That's the land for me!
I'm going to Sacramento
With my washbowl on my knee.

This, with infinite variations, became the theme song of the forty-niners. It was not long before foreign voices were heard in chorus; with astonishing speed, multitudes from all parts of the world joined Americans in their migration. Before 1849 was out, guidebooks were appearing in various languages of Europe (for example, *Californiens Gegenwart und Zukunft* in Berlin, *Gids Naar California* in Amsterdam) as well as texts in English published as far apart as London and Sydney. Presently, strange names appeared on the topography of California, to remind posterity what manner of men had sought their fortunes up there: Malakoff Diggings, Dutch Flat, French Corral, Kanaka Creek and many more.

The seekers of gold were later to be known as the Argonauts, though not many, perhaps, would have identified themselves as such. The name was to be much bandied about by less robust but more literary souls, who enjoyed wallowing in a good classical allusion whenever they could spot one. Some anonymous hand, writing in the *Californian*, a San Francisco weekly that Bret Harte helped to start in 1863, seems to have made the first suggestion that in the Gold Rush lay a splendid theme for a revised version of the golden fleece legend, with Sam Brannan cast as Jason.

Harte founded his own writing career on a short acquaintance with the goldminers. Coming to California in 1854, he worked for a time as a schoolmaster in one of the mining settlements, where he picked up the material for short stories and the verses that eventually made him the leading man of letters in the West. As an editor of the *Californian*, he published some early pieces by Mark Twain, who came to San Francisco in 1864 and in one year learned enough about the goldfields to secure his own reputation with stories like "The Celebrated Jumping Frog of Calaveras County", inspired by a bit of gossip he heard around Ben Coon's bar-room stove up in Angel's Camp.

The Argonauts themselves started by panning for gold in the beds of a hundred streams, laboriously swirling pay dirt in the water so that the heavy gold particles would sink to the bottom of the pan and separate from the lighter dross. A hard worker could process perhaps 50 pans in a day; by then his back would be breaking and his rheumatism would be giving him hell—and he might well have found no gold. Before long, however, the labour-saving rocker box was devised; and after that the so-called Long Tom, and later still the sluice box. All consisted essentially of a

Two of the most popular stage performers to entertain the prospectors of the gold camps were the erotic dancer Lola Montez (above) and her protégée Lotta Crabtree (right), who rose from child stardom to become a celebrated comedienne in New York, London and Paris.

wooden contraption with a sieve and a catchment device, into which the dirt was shovelled and agitated after water had been poured over it.

But the most efficient method of extracting gold from the hills was hydraulic mining, introduced in 1853. The procedure was very simple. You just hosed away the hillside with a high-velocity jet of water shot from a large nozzle, washing the dirt down to a series of large sluice boxes that trapped the gold. The biggest nozzles were nine inches in diameter and expelled 30,000 gallons a minute. In order to get the water from the nearest river a system of flumes and ditches was required. In the end, something like 5,000 miles of artificial water coursing was spread across El Dorado. The hosing itself changed the landscape, as you can see today if you go up to the Malakoff Diggings, where the bare gravels of the hillside rise in ribs and gullies, empty of any signs of life. Below, the serrated ground is thick with sage and other tangled growths that conceal pieces of the iron tools the miners left around. But birds do not sing there any more and the place seems haunted by many ghosts.

This devastation of the land was the everlasting price of the most profitable operations, though miners who made fortunes were few and far between. At one time it was reckoned that one man, at the Rich Dry Diggings, was finding $15,000 a day while others nearby were delighted to take just $100. But the majority of men, in the long run, counted themselves lucky to have averaged $5 a day. Plenty of them went home discouraged after months or even years up in the hills, having done no more than cover their expenses. Yet at the height of the Gold Rush, so many men were working these hills that, cumulatively, their labours produced metal on a scale to defeat the imagination. More than $4 million worth a month was still being shipped out of San Francisco at the end of 1858, when the Rush was well past its peak. As always, it was the middlemen who consistently made the biggest fortunes in this boom.

Those who struck it dramatically rich were the ones who came early and stayed behind in San Francisco to earn their living by commerce. In 1849, eggs were sold in town at a dollar apiece; wooden houses, knocked together on the cheap, were rented for $800 a month. At first, the entrepreneurs may have been selling only simple necessities of food, shelter and equipment to men bound for the goldfields, but before long they were making much of their money from the fast-expanding community of San Francisco itself. Before the end of 1850, the 900 inhabitants galvanized by Sam Brannan's immortal news had become 25,000.

Men of initiative could generate fortunes from the smallest beginnings. Peter Donahue came to town in 1849 and set up his Union Iron Works with a little forge and $100 worth of tools to manufacture miners' pans and other implements; 10 years later he had machinery worth $150,000, a work-force of 120 men and was handling a contract for the U.S. Navy that would net him $75,000. The year 1850 saw the arrival of Levi Strauss, a

Bavarian who had migrated to New York before joining the Gold Rush. He was a dry-goods dealer by trade and entered the Golden Gate with yards of heavy cloth, needles and thread, and a plan to cash in on the need for tenting out in the hills. Finding that durable clothing was in even shorter supply than shelter, he adapted his materials to making heavy-duty pants whose stress points were reinforced with small metal rivets—an enterprise that was to grow into an enormous international trade.

Another early arrival whose name would become inseparable from San Francisco's was Domingo Ghirardelli, an Italian, who had discovered chocolate in Guatemala. Improbably, he headed for California to sell the strange new sweet to the miners from tent stores. Before long, he was also processing mustard, coffee and spices from a brick building on the waterfront. It still stands today, rearranged by history and the preservationists, so that when you sail through the Golden Gate, one of the first things you see to starboard after rounding Fort Point is the name of Ghirardelli picked out in large neon lights.

There were many others like these men, and commerce of all kinds was soon thriving on the Bay. By 1852, San Francisco contained a score of clothing stores and 63 bakeries, more than 160 hotels and restaurants, two dozen bath houses, 19 banks—and bars and gambling places galore.

It was still a primitive place, though, with streets that turned into seas of mud after a heavy rain, so that drunks sometimes fell down in a stupor and drowned. William Tecumseh Sherman—a soldier destined to win general's rank during the Civil War and later to command all U.S. forces in the West during the Indian wars—decided in the course of a visit that San Francisco was not built for cavalry. "Montgomery Street," he wrote after trying to negotiate its inclines in the spring of 1850, "had been filled up with brush and clay, and I always dreaded to ride on horseback along it." Kearny Street was "not even jackassable" for most of its length, though an attempt had been made to firm up 25 yards of it by dumping sacks of flour and bran, bales of tobacco, pieces of stoves and an old piano into the quagmire. A physician who came to town at this time had even worse things to report—rotted food and the intestines of slaughtered animals thrown out into streets and yards. It was, he announced, "the most abhorrent place that man ever lived in".

On the other hand, there was no lack of diversions. By 1852, horse-racing had become so popular at a track near the Mission Dolores that animals of quality were being imported from Australia. The hedonist spirit that the earliest arrivals from the East had detected in the natives of Yerba Buena—and which has always been inseparable from San Francisco—was boundless during the period of the Gold Rush. Before the *California* steamed into the Bay, Joseph Rowe's Olympic Circus had come to town and was performing on Kearny Street under a big top that could accommodate 1,500 people; and the Eagle Theatre Company was

Sam Brannan—Mormon preacher, land speculator, store-keeper, newspaper owner and drunk—was a notable exponent of self-help during the Gold Rush. In 1851, angered by the lawlessness then sweeping San Francisco, he and two others set up a 600-man-strong Committee of Vigilance to police the streets. By the time it disbanded a year later, the committee had lynched four felons and brought a temporary peace to the city.

Artillerymen stand by a cannon positioned on the roof and sentries patrol the sandbagged approaches to "Fort Gunnybags", the stronghold of the city's second Committee of Vigilance. Formed in 1856 after the murder of a newspaper editor, the committee tried and hanged four men, deported 30 troublemakers, defied the state militia and after restoring law and order in three months, disbanded with a final march-past of more than 6,000 armed men.

playing straight drama in Washington Hall above Foley's Saloon. It was not long before San Francisco's resident population, as well as the miners coming and going between the Bay and the goldfields, could pick and choose among the attractions of Rowe's troupe and such entertainment centres as the Eagles, the Lyric Casino, the Gaieties, the Varieties and more, including a second circus that had been started by one of Joseph Rowe's clowns. But the most typical entertainments were the saloons of Portsmouth Square, where the roulette wheels were kept spinning and the booze flowed in torrents by day and by night.

There were relatively few women in San Francisco at the beginning of 1849, and the miners who passed through on the way to the fields could sometimes be caught with faraway, haunted looks when they saw a child playing by the road. But an unbending toughness was nonetheless a hallmark of the town—and even more so of the goldfields. No law existed up in the hills except the law of crude retribution for the quickly taken offence. Claim-jumping meant flogging and banishment from the area, and a thief often had his ears cropped before being sent on his way. Lynchings became common from the beginning of 1849, when three men were hanged by a kangaroo court not far from Coloma where the whole saga had begun. Knife fights and gun play were ordinary events in the course of any day. The rough justice of the times is also memorialized in the names given to the gold camps: Hangtown, Chicken Thief Flat, Cut Throat Bar, Garrotte and Second Garrotte.

As the foreigners rolled in, the very nastiest forms of lawlessness occurred, based on racial hatred. By the middle of 1849, a gang called the Hounds had been unleashed in San Francisco; they were known thus because they hounded Mexicans, Peruvians and anyone else without a white skin who had ventured into a land that, as they put it, had been "preserved by nature for Americans only, who possess noble hearts". The Hounds were the remnants of a New York regiment that had fought in the war with Mexico and had been disbanded in California by Colonel J. D. Stevenson, who went into land speculation there. Under an ex-lieutenant, Sam Roberts, they became a self-appointed police force, paid by ship-owners to retrieve sailors who had deserted to the goldfields. But then they turned their attention to the growing Latin quarter of San Francisco, raiding it in garish uniforms of their own design, to the sound of fife and drum, plundering, raping and terrorizing as they went. Their heyday was a short one, as was that of a hoodlum gang that arrived from Australia, styled themselves the Sydney Ducks, and made the waterfront the scene of their protection rackets and any other violence that would pay.

What finished the Hounds and later the Ducks was the outrage of San Francisco's merchants, who decided to take law and order into their own hands under the leadership of Sam Brannan. San Francisco's first Vigilance Committee was formed one night in the summer of 1851 and went to work just hours later. A thief named John Jenkins—a member of the Sydney Ducks—had been surprised in a shipping agent's office and caught after a chase; but instead of being placed in the custody of the law officers who answered to San Francisco's mayor, he was handed over to the Vigilance Committee. The members tried him in quick time, pronounced him guilty and, by two in the morning, had the remains of poor Jenkins swinging from a rope in Portsmouth Square.

The coroner's inquest was highly critical of this procedure until the entire committee of 183 citizens insisted on taking joint responsibility; whereupon legal law enforcement in San Francisco backed down for the time being. Before the month was out, the committee was 500 strong and the Reverend Timothy Hunt was preaching its virtues from his pulpit. The committee was disbanded after 100 days in the face of a con-demnation from the mayor and an even stronger one from the local judiciary. But four years later, incensed by the recurring lawlessness of the town (there were 1,000 murders in San Francisco between 1849 and 1856), the respectable citizenry again attempted to take matters into their own hands. The second Vigilance Committee was a para-military force that grew to 6,000 armed men in the four months of its existence. It con-fined its hangings to murderers, and it ingeniously expelled the most in-corrigible petty criminals by the simple expedient of booking and paying for their passages out through the Golden Gate: thus Billy Mulligan, Yankee Sullivan and Martin Gallagher were ordered out for being "disturbers of the peace of our city, destroyers of the purity of our elections, active members and leaders of the organized gangs who have invaded the sanctity of our ballot boxes, and perfect pests to Society".

A cleansing process, no doubt—but the vigilantes could not for long be tolerated by lawful government. When California's young Governor J. Neely Johnson made it clear that he was prepared to muster troops against them and asked President Pierce for arms and ammunition in support, the vigilantes disbanded once more. But the streets of San Francisco were draped with flags and loud with cheers as they paraded with bands, horsemen and artillery for the last time, on August 18, 1856.

By then, the most sensational period of the Gold Rush was over. Though the precious metal continued to be hosed out of the El Dorado hills in great quantity for several years to come, thousands of miners would soon abandon those diggings to try their fortunes at new fields in British Columbia and to scrabble for silver in Nevada's Comstock Lode—a stupendously rich strike made on the far side of the Sierra.

It is still possible to catch a whiff of those times in San Francisco today. No longer, perhaps, in Portsmouth Square, where bedlam reigns only at the Chinese New Year, being otherwise the province of elderly gentlemen who sit at tables under trees and are rapt in contemplation of the next move at checkers or a game of mah-jong. No longer, even, in the modern commerce of shipping around the Bay, for that proceeds without haste and with a smooth electrical hum across waters that (it is said) still conceal the remains of many abandoned Gold-Rush hulks. But go into some of the waterfront bars and watch the challenge in the air as a customer prepares to order a drink. "Will you shake?" he asks the barman, nodding towards the dice and leather cup, half hidden in shadow beside the beer pump. With a surreptitious glance (for shaking is not quite within the law) the barman brings them out and casts the dice upon the bar. If he wins, the customer pays double; if not, the drink is free. And that, unless I'm much mistaken, is the living spirit of the Argonauts at work.

3

Stop-and-Go Symphony

There is something wayward, and irresistibly appealing, about a city that is prepared to lose a million dollars a year on a conveyance with little to be said for it apart from its charm. To keep its cable cars running along a mere half dozen of its streets, San Francisco is not only willing to do that for a year or two, but has virtually guaranteed it will cover the deficit for all time to come. In 1955, the citizenry added to the City Charter a clause stating that never, but never, would the cable cars be allowed to disappear—and not a word of that clause may be altered unless a majority of San Francisco's voters say so. In a world of increasingly hardheaded taxpayers, this is no small triumph of the human spirit and, as far as I'm concerned, San Francisco is fully entitled to its reward from the tourist trade, without which the municipal book-keeping might well be wrecked beyond repair.

As an everyday mode of transportation, cable cars—propelled by a cable moving under the road—ceased to make much sense once automobiles and buses arrived to tackle the hills in less restrained style. Nevertheless, San Franciscans in large numbers continue to use them—partly, I suspect, out of sheer sentiment. Even in seasons when tourists are scarce, the cable cars can be crowded on any of the three lines, particularly during the rush hours.

At times of peak traffic, you will observe that the employees of the San Francisco Municipal Railway—which operates all three lines—are among the most amiable of men. Consider this typical scene. A cable car on the Powell-Hyde Line grinds to a hilltop stage. The car is already full of passengers, beyond the notional limit of 40 or so, and a dozen more are now hoping to get on. The gripman—so-called because he controls the "grip" by which the car is connected to the cable—reckons they have been waiting long enough. He calls out: "Let's move right down inside now, so all these good people can get on, too." Those inside cram closer together, with apologetic nods and understanding smiles, for the gripman's affability is infectious as well as imperative. And somehow the others do manage to get aboard, even though most of them are perched on the wet and windy running-boards, holding on desperately in one of San Francisco's minor but most bracing sports.

Draughtiness is by no means the only imperfection of the cable cars. They are also apt to make life difficult for motorists, who, after all, have enough on their minds merely trying to negotiate San Francisco's steep hills, without having to stop *en route*—as local law ordains—every time a cable car halts in front of them. Even worse, the vehicles sometimes lose

As thick morning fog rolls in from the Pacific, rush-hour motorists switch on their headlights while crossing the Golden Gate Bridge into San Francisco. The six-lane bridge, which links the city with Marin County, carries an average of more than 100,000 cars a day.

their grip on the cable, causing a safety device to take charge and bring the car to a jolting halt. Such breakdowns—which may require an hour or so of repair work—happen rather a lot on the corner of Washington and Jackson, where the Powell-Hyde and the Powell-Mason cars cross at right angles on their way from Market Street to the waterfront; and the other traffic then has to make what shifts it can in trying to get around the contraptions blocking the middle of the road. But drivers tend to accept these obstructions equably, with wry grins. Cable cars, after all, belong.

It is said that the cable car came to San Francisco because Andrew S. Hallidie—owner of a wire, rope and cable company that had been doing very well manufacturing aerial ropeways to convey ore out of the gold and silver mines of the Sierra Nevada—witnessed an accident to a horsedrawn tram in 1869. One of the four horses pulling the tram up a slope stumbled and, when the brakes failed, the vehicle rolled down the hill, taking the terrified animals with it. Hallidie was so moved by compassion for the horses that he decided to produce an alternative form of transport—a trolley that would clamp on to a continuously travelling cable when it was required to move, and would release its grip on the wire when it needed to stop. The wire itself would be propelled by a steam-engine housed in a shed. San Franciscans have long called this powerhouse "The Barn"; you can visit it today and see the miles of cable for the three existing lines winding in perpetual motion over 14-foot wheels before disappearing outside into channels beneath the street.

Hallidie's inspiration relied heavily on the brains of an engineer called Benjamin C. Brook; and if Brook had been able to get financial backing of his own, he would doubtless be regarded today as the father of the San Francisco cable car. But Hallidie's claim to the invention is at least fortified by his display of nerve when the trial run took place, in the face of ridicule from the citizenry at large. He stepped into his first trolley at the top end—not the bottom—of Clay Street, thus facing the possibility that he might be carried by a runaway down six blocks of a very steep hill. Instead, he descended calmly at an impeccable nine miles per hour, which has remained the regulation speed ever since. After that, there was no holding the rush to make cable cars for San Francisco. By 1890, eight different companies were running this form of transport in the city; and nowhere in the world has it ever been as fashionable as here.

The cable cars represent more than a rather cumbersome way of shifting some 25,000 people a day across 10 miles of streets. As they lumber up and down those hills and trundle across the level places in between, they are a genuine glimpse of the past, a patina of age upon a city that is still young. They say much about the spirit of the city's inhabitants, quite apart from the perpetual debt San Franciscans are prepared to sustain to keep them in operation. For one thing, all official notices in the cars—prohibiting smoking or the playing of radios, for example—are preceded by "Please".

While company employees stand by, passengers wait aboard a tram operated in the 1870s by San Francisco's first cable-car line, the Clay Street Hill Railroad. Such cars, seating 12 people, carried the controls (visible in the middle of the car) and usually had a larger passenger transporter hitched up behind.

Perhaps in response to this civilized tone, the old-fashioned liveries of the three surviving lines have been unmolested by the graffiti of the young. True, I have detected "H. Bogart rode on this car circa 1946-7" written in an unsteady hand on one vehicle of the Powell-Hyde line; but that is not so much graffiti as a battle honour of sorts. The cable cars themselves are a battle honour in a country that is constantly demanding new and more expensive toys—some of which, as we shall presently see, do not work as well. Everything about these old cars adds up to an exhibition of character. "Let's all get close together inside, then," the gripman shouts. "I know it's an un-American activity, but let's give it a try." No wonder San Francisco has held on to the damned awkward things.

The Golden Gate Bridge is the other image of San Francisco best known to the world outside, and another object held close to the affections of its people. It is not, to my mind, the most exciting of the local bridges to cross. As a driver, I much prefer the Bay Bridge connecting with Oakland; it pours you downhill, along its top deck, straight into the heart of the city. The Golden Gate Bridge cannot claim the distinction of seniority (the Dumbarton Drawbridge, connecting San Mateo and Alameda Counties, preceded it by a decade), nor is it the longest bridge across San Francisco Bay (the San Mateo Bridge is 7.2 miles long; the Golden Gate, less than two miles in length). Where the Golden Gate scores above all the other bridges is in the delicacy of its design and the relation of that design to the spectacular gap the bridge traverses on the edge of the Pacific Ocean.

When fogs come in and slip over its deck, the Golden Gate Bridge becomes as beautiful as any of the great natural wonders of the world.

Perched more than 200 feet above San Francisco Bay, two helmeted workers attach cables to a hoist during construction of the Golden Gate Bridge in the 1930s.

But even on the clearest days there is something about the slimness of the steelwork and the curve of the suspension cables that make you gasp for the bridge's survival. The best view I know is from Alcatraz; if you look towards the open sea from the island in the middle of the Bay, the bridge seems to hang distantly in space like a fragile slip of filigree. It almost spoils the effect to know that those cables are three feet in diameter; it helps the illusion of fragility if you recall that each was spun from 27,000 strands of wire, not one of them thicker than a pencil lead.

Although today the inland sea is spanned by no fewer than five bridges, nothing but boats crossed these waters until the 1920s. During the early decades of this century, the ferries were even more a part of San Francisco's life than the cable cars, though they were always discreetly in the background, lying at the waterfront after bringing large numbers of people to work in the city, or taking even larger numbers to labour in the plants of Oakland and other industrial areas on the east side of the Bay. The ferry boat owners, predictably enough, were vehemently against bridges when construction was first proposed. So too, when the question of the Golden Gate Bridge first arose, were the shipowners, who argued that the thing would only bottle up the harbour and do the city no good. They failed to stop the project because too many citizens were tired of being weatherbound on distant shores when the ferries were unable to sail— and also because A. P. Giannini was prepared to back the venture with the millions in his Bank of America.

The author of the scheme to bridge the mouth of the Bay was Joseph Baermann Strauss who, when he first made the suggestion in 1918, had already put a bridge across Russia's Neva River at St. Petersburg, as well as designing the central span for the Arlington Main Bridge in Washington, D.C. Anyone who designs bridges is by profession a dreamer, with the rare privilege of actually being able to build his castles in the air. Strauss was even more visionary than most, having as a young man produced a graduate thesis in engineering that proposed the joining of North America to Asia with a bridge across the Bering Strait. His plan for the Golden Gate Bridge was almost as startling, and the voters of six coastal counties did not approve the necessary bonds to finance the project until 1930. Two more years passed before work actually began.

Building the north pier turned out to be relatively easy, since solid rock descended to the water's edge on that side. But creating the San Francisco terminus of the bridge was a much greater challenge: because there was no rock on the shore, the pier had to be constructed on a submarine shelf some distance into the channel beyond Fort Point. Sceptics had always reckoned this an impossible thing to do in the powerful currents that sweep back and forth between the Pacific and the Bay; and you can see what they meant if you go down to Fort Point now and watch the surfers ride high breakers right alongside the south pier. The current is so strong that Strauss's divers could work only between tides—one hour at a time, four times a day—to plant dynamite on the shelf for the foundation work. When a floating trestle was built to position equipment over the place where the pier would be lodged, the workmen became seasick in swells that were sometimes 15 feet high—and that was the least of the difficulties with the trestle. A freighter rammed the structure in fog and sank 100 feet of it. Three months later, heavy seas battered the rebuilt trestle, knocked off equipment and sank three concrete blocks, each the size of a house, that were intended to be pier foundations.

Strauss eventually countered the currents by erecting a concrete wall around the site, so that his men could work in still water. The barrier was 30 feet thick and five storeys high, but when the first caisson was towed in, a storm blew up, the two massive objects were banged together, and the concrete wall was smashed. Strauss rebuilt the barrier, pumped out the water, laid a concrete floor 40 feet thick and, in the middle of that turbulent channel, created a dry area the size of a football field. On this, at last, the south pier began to take shape.

For myself, Strauss's greatest triumph was not so much the bridge as the fact that in the first four years of work, in terrible conditions, not one man was killed. He was meticulous in taking safety precautions. When the time came to put in the suspension cables, the riggers were given special diets to counteract dizziness (they were also supplied with sauerkraut juice to clear hangovers), and they wore special goggles to prevent sun blindness in the glare that develops when the fog banks roll up. Strauss also thought it worth spending $80,000 on a safety net, and the 19 men who tumbled into it and bounced up again in one piece formed a "Halfway to Hell" club to celebrate still being alive.

This remarkable safety record lasted until a few months before the bridge was finished. Then a derrick toppled on the deck, killing a man. A few weeks before the last work was done, a dozen men were standing on a temporary platform below the bridge deck and its newly laid concrete roadway. A bracket holding the platform snapped and the whole thing plunged through the safety net, which could not bear the weight. Nine men died at once and their bodies were swept out to sea. Two were rescued from the water, and one man was hauled to safety from under the deck itself: he had grabbed at something as the platform fell and hung there, legs dangling in space, his pipe still clenched firmly between his teeth.

On opening day, May 27, 1937, 202,000 people walked across the bridge to enjoy the sensation of hanging securely in space, and it is still possible to do that along the pedestrian lanes on either side. The motorist, however, has other things to watch—not least, the amount of buffeting he is getting from the wind, which can swerve a car across three lanes if a storm is blowing in from the Pacific. Only once has the bridge been closed because of bad weather, and that was a quarter of a century ago; a wind blew so unpredictably strongly from the south-west (an unlikely quarter at any force) that the deck began to oscillate in great waves along the whole of its length, so that one rail would rise 11 feet above the other, then reverse positions a moment later as the wave moved on. But the bridge held; Strauss had designed it to withstand hurricane winds even if vehicles were jammed bumper to bumper in all six lanes and pedestrians were packed like sardines along the outside tracks.

Time seems to have proved the soundness of his daring design. In spite of the treacherous waters flowing beneath the bridge, there has always been ample room between its piers for shipping to manoeuvre and pass. As for the room between the underside of the deck and the sea's surface, it ranges from 220 to 240 feet, depending on the state of the tide, the heat of the day and the amount of traffic crossing the bridge. Just once has there been a really close shave: when the *Queen Elizabeth* steamed into San Francisco as a troopship during the Second World War and her topmast cleared the roadway with no more than a couple of feet to spare.

The only disasters here have been sad and private ones, for well over 600 people have jumped from the Golden Gate Bridge to their deaths. An analysis of this toll by the San Francisco Suicide Prevention Bureau has revealed some striking patterns: nearly three-quarters of the suicides have been men; most go on a Tuesday; and May and October appear to be the likeliest months. There is a strong local belief that, whenever the suicides occur, the majority of people climb over the rail on the eastern side, where they can take a last look at the city before they jump.

Sometimes would-be suicides are intercepted before they can do themselves harm; closed circuit television enables officials at the toll booths to keep watch on the whole length of the bridge and send a highway patrolman to have a word with any disconsolate figure who lingers too long at the rail. But every year there are those who evade the watchers of the Golden Gate, making the bridge a symbol of the worst as well as the best in this city. It is a monument to the questing spirit that has vitalized San Francisco from the start; but it can also be the fatal beauty, the last attraction to those whose staying power has finally been spent.

The year Andrew Hallidie was moved to develop San Francisco's cable cars, a much more potent event occurred some distance to the east. In May, 1869, at Promontory, Utah, the completion of the nation's first transcontinental railroad was signalled by the ceremonial driving of a golden spike—and San Francisco entered a new era. If the Gold Rush put the city on its feet, the railroad ensured it would never need to look back. Gold production had, in fact, slumped in the 1860s, but at the very moment it began to wane, new wealth was discovered in the silver deposits of Nevada. The railroad was San Francisco's means of exploiting that bonanza more effectively than before, just as it was Eastern America's

Dumbarton Bridge, 1927.

San Mateo Bridge, 1956.

Four long toll bridges, both suspension and cantilever types, cross San Francisco Bay and the adjacent San Pablo Bay lying to its north. Ranging in length from the 4.7-mile span of the Dumbarton Bridge—first to be built—to the San Mateo Bridge's 7.2-mile sweep, they helped open the whole Bay area to industry and commerce.

San Francisco-Oakland Bay Bridge, 1936.

Richmond-San Rafael Bridge (with oil pipeline in foreground), 1956.

opportunity to tap this inordinate wealth in the West. Abraham Lincoln had been encouraged to sign the Pacific Railroad Act in 1862 because he wanted gold and silver for the coffers of the Union.

Even more important for San Francisco was the access the city now had to markets in the East. Moreover, trade with the Orient was opening up and San Francisco—with her marvellous harbour—was perfectly situated to be the entrepôt for two continents. The value of exports from that harbour had stood at $8 million in 1860. By 1875 they were worth $33 million; and by 1889 they rose to $47 million. Transporting goods across the ocean to and from San Francisco had been no problem at all; moving them quickly and in bulk between the city and the eastern states was a hopeless proposition until the Union Pacific (the eastern section of the transcontinental railroad) and the Central Pacific (the western section, with San Francisco at its end) met at Promontory.

The true father of the Central Pacific was an engineer named Theodore Judah, who had built California's first line up the Sacramento Valley in 1854, before he reached the age of thirty. His vision of a transcontinental line had taken him to the political lobbies of Washington as well as to the wealthy potential backers of San Francisco. In neither case had he received the encouragement he was after. He finally got the support he needed from a handful of modestly successful businessmen in Sacramento; these men had made their money from the sale of goods to mining townships in the Sierra, and they were eager that Judah's railroad should assist them to make more. They were not very interested in the line going further east— until, in 1862, federal grants were offered to subsidize the transcontinental link, and the Sacramento businessmen discovered that applicants could virtually name their own figure for these: you could collect money from Washington by claiming to have levelled a hillside at inordinate expense where no hillside existed—and officials in Washington were too far away to check the veracity of the claim. By then Judah had died, leaving behind his engineering plans, his route maps and his valuable contacts in Washington. On that foundation, and on their own unscrupulous greed, the small-town businessmen became multi-millionaires. Judah's widow never received a cent of their profits.

They were to be known as the Big Four. Collis P. Huntington was the dominant figure; Mark Hopkins was his yes-man; Leland Stanford was the greediest of the lot; and Charles Crocker was the big fixer. They had come from the East individually, during the Gold Rush, and for a short time Crocker had actually dirtied his hands in the mines. They were not all good friends. The austere Huntington and the flamboyant Stanford loathed each other. Huntington spent five years of their business alliance preparing to expose the election-rigging by which Stanford won himself a seat in the United States Senate. But the Big Four worked marvellously well together in making joint fortunes and ruthlessly smashing any opposition.

Stanford, Hopkins and Huntington manipulated politicians to serve their purposes in both Washington and Sacramento—where Stanford served a term as California's Governor. Crocker attended to the work in the field, bringing thousands of coolies across from China to chisel a route out of the Sierra rock, for minimal wages.

When their east-bound Central Pacific had been joined to the west-bound Union Pacific and the transcontinental line was at last a reality, the Big Four set about acquiring a West Coast monopoly of commercial traffic on a scale to stagger even San Francisco's vivid imagination. Having become vastly rich by milking the federal government of its railroad subsidies, they now increased their wealth by purchasing all the local railroad lines they did not already own. The Central Pacific bought up the Oakland waterfront and much of that of San Francisco to provide itself with a base for commerce with the Orient. In the end, the Big Four also controlled virtually all water transport around the Bay, all river traffic into the hinterland, and much of the shipping overseas.

If a straight business transaction on terms advantageous to the Big Four could not be arranged, then bribery and worse got them what they wanted. Municipal elections were rigged as a matter of course. Having acquired their monopoly on the transport of goods in the West and over much of the ocean beyond, they fixed the traffic rates at any level they pleased, taking plunder on a scale unheard of since the Middle Ages. Inevitably, they were detested for their ruthless efficiency. Newspapers of the time caricatured the Big Four as an octopus and, although they were all dead by 1901, the tentacles of the beast they created held on to its monopoly until the federal government dismembered it in 1913.

The most celebrated evidence of their wealth were the mansions, of preposterous size and conspicuous vulgarity, they built on top of Nob Hill. The Huntington house was designed in the style of a French château, the Crocker residence in a sort of Bavarian fretwork with a tower 76 feet high. Leland Stanford's home had signs of the zodiac inlaid in black marble on the floor and a picture gallery in which, at the press of a button, plants would rise from concealment and fill the air with the song of mechanical birds perched among the foliage. At Mark Hopkins' place, the drawing room was known as the Palace of the Doges; and the master bedroom was restless with ebony, ivory and inlaid jewels. Hopkins himself scarcely got to know his turreted eyesore; he died in 1878, leaving it and much else to a widow who swiftly became a public figure on her own account by reason of a private life that was erroneously believed to be all-embracing. She did, however, become infatuated with an interior decorator more than twenty years her junior. When they married, she disinherited her adopted son in favour of the new husband and, amidst much publicity, young Timothy Hopkins sued successfully for several million dollars. All this was no more than the spirit of the age San Francisco was then going through.

Shaded according to stages of evaporation, flats that produce crude salt for tanning, pickling and other uses form part of the industrial belt girdling the Bay.

The railroad barons themselves were nothing less than tokens of the times. The *Élite Directory* of 1879 disclosed an upper crust of San Francisco society 6,000 families thick, and there were many imitations of those mansions on Nob Hill. A private stable was an invariable adjunct of each; and more than one of them sheltered the master's horses on mosaic floors beneath the light of crystal chandeliers.

At this level of society, balls and parties of every description were held on any pretext, the most desirable pretext of all being the arrival of any-body, from any corner of the globe, with royal or merely noble blood. There was an endless procession of such characters—Japanese princesses, the Emperor of Brazil, Queen Victoria's daughter, Lord and Lady Dufferin, Admiral Farragut; and the Hawaiian King Kalakaua appeared more than once, and finally expired in his customary suite in the Palace Hotel. It was an age when well-bred San Francisco daughters hoped to marry even better-bred birds of passage, as many of them did. Flora Sharon got the Baronet Thomas George Fermor-Hesketh; Virginia Bonynge picked up Viscount Deerhurst; and the two Holladay girls bagged a brace in the persons of Baron de Boussière and the Comte de Pourtalès.

A bit further down the social scale life was also humming, as San Francisco bounded towards the 20th Century to the steady rhythm of the railroad's beat. By the 1890s, the city had more than 3,000 establishments licensed to sell liquor, and another 2,000 places that served the same purpose illegally. Many of these were ranged along the alleyways of the Barbary Coast, a raddled stretch of the city that ran from the waterfront to Broadway, where sailors in the Gold-Rush days had gathered at the Boar's Head, the Fierce Grizzly and other taverns of their choice. But something more sophisticated became the general order of the day all over San Francisco. At Johnny Farley's Peerless Saloon you could try one of the new iced cocktails, like a Gold Rush Sazerac (a shot of rye, with bitters, absinthe and anisette). The Bank Exchange Bar offered Pisco Punch, with Peruvian brandy as an explosive base. Every day the streets of San Francisco were awash with strollers who appeared to have no other purpose in life but to move from one establishment to another. Money came easy and was spent with such a splash that many saloons threw in a free lunch. At the Bank Exchange Bar you could take your pick of anything from clams and oysters to turkey and pigs' heads, from crab legs in sherry to terrapin stew.

Prostitution was big business at all hours of the day and night. The city directories openly listed so-called boarding houses manned by "seam-stresses" galore—the largest of such establishments being the Nymphia, a three-storey tenement that could cater to 450 clients at a time, with the girls working a system of double shifts. Many and illustrious were the town's Madams. Though few could match Tessie Wall, who married the gambler Frank Deroux. On the night of their first encounter she downed 22 bottles of champagne without once leaving the room; much

Charles Crocker, one of the 19th-Century railroad barons, leaves a trail of havoc as he skates in caricature through Golden Gate Park on a pair of scaled-down tramcars. The cartoon, from a contemporary satirical journal called the "Wasp", was provoked by Crocker's scheme to run a tramline through the park. Rich, ruthless and influential, he managed to obtain the support of the San Francisco Board of Supervisors, though eventually the scheme was vetoed by the Mayor.

At Fisherman's Wharf, a large sign beckons tourists to board one of the sightseeing vessels that sails around San Francisco Bay. The 75-minute excursion will take them past Alcatraz Island, up to the Golden Gate Bridge, down to the Bay Bridge and finally back to the pier.

later, alas, she pumped his body full of lead because he wanted a divorce.

There were, of course, quieter pleasures than any of these. The Bay City Wheelmen were regularly to be seen bicycling across the new Golden Gate Park, which John McLaren was creating out of sandhills by the Pacific shore. At Adolph Sutro's Baths, 1,000 bathers at a time could disport themselves in any one of six glass tanks at temperatures between 50° and 110°F. But neither cyclists nor bathers figured high in the reasons why San Francisco, by the 1890s, had become chief rival to Paris as The Wickedest City in the World, and why Oscar Wilde, contemplating its headlong hedonism from a distance, dryly remarked that "anyone who has disappeared is said to have been seen in San Francisco".

In several ways San Francisco would never be the same after that epoch, and nowhere do you get a sense of the decline in its fortunes more clearly than when you contemplate the port—the Embarcadero—today. It occupies the edge of the city that curves around into San Francisco Bay, starting from Fisherman's Wharf opposite Alcatraz and continuing in an arc well past the Oakland Bay Bridge. To say that Fisherman's Wharf is by far the liveliest stretch of that arc is to make the most depressing comment possible on the state of the port as a whole; the wharf is nothing much more than a catchpenny title that attracts a lot of tourists to eating places of uneven distinction, and to various subsidiary sideshows—fishermen and their boats being heavily outnumbered by landlubbers who know how to make a fast buck. Behind the wharf, a more elegant commerce flourishes

Commuters from Marin County step off a ferry at the Embarcadero terminal. Discontinued in 1938, soon after the opening of the Golden Gate Bridge, the ferry service was brought back into operation in 1970 to help relieve the growing pressure on road traffic.

around Ghirardelli Square and The Cannery shopping complex. But beyond, where the Embarcadero thrusts into the water the first of its long sequence of piers, and the old Ferry Building and its clock poke up in the shadow of the aerial freeway, the waterfront is sadly in decline. Most of the piers are inactive now, and the road that runs past them is by and large a ruin of potholes and bad patches, with little heavy traffic on it. And no wonder: from Telegraph Hill above, you can see that the cargo-vessels entering San Francisco Bay usually sail right past the Embarcadero, bound for destinations on the further shore.

Yet the port, with the Gold Rush and the railroad, was chiefly responsible for the making of San Francisco. A whole segment of America's maritime history was bound up here, beginning in the days when the clippers of the Comstock Line, Winsor's Regular Line, Glidden and Williams' Line and Coleman's California Line clapped on all sail to carry Argonauts from the Eastern seaboard to this port. There might have been periodic lulls in the remarkable vitality of the port, but they were always followed by another great leap ahead. The aftermath of the Gold Rush left a scarred landscape, crumbling mines and a forest of abandoned masts, but by 1900 the railroad had transformed San Francisco into the third busiest harbour in the world. By then, the traffic in clipper ships had given way to steam, and the markings of Coleman, Comstock and the rest had been supplanted by those of Dollar, Matson, United Fruit, American-Hawaiian and several more.

In 1914 another lift came with the opening of the Panama Canal, which made direct shipping from Europe and the east coast of South America a more attractive possibility. In spite of the Great Depression and its turbulent times along the waterfront, San Francisco was still more than holding its own when the Second World War came. At that time, no fewer than 175 steamship companies were regularly using the Embarcadero piers. San Francisco was the fourth busiest port in the United States and the unquestioned leader in the West.

It now ranks fifth among the 20 shipping harbours strung along the American Pacific coast. The Port of Los Angeles-Long Beach is the leader these days; but San Diego, Seattle and Oakland are also ahead of San Francisco. Almost every year since the war, the tonnage of shipping moving in and out of San Francisco has declined. In 1946, the port handled more than seven million tons; 30 years later the figure had dropped to less than two and a half million tons. What rankles with San Francisco is that while its port has been in decline, Oakland's has been expanding steadily. It is possible to shrug one's shoulders philosophically at the advance of Los Angeles-Long Beach, which owes much of its success to the area's larger population (among other things, this means that many more Japanese ships laden with Japanese cars are likely to dock down there). But to give way to Oakland is another matter.

There are several reasons why the traditional rivalry between the two ports has gone Oakland's way. One of them—geography—is quite outside San Francisco's control. Two railroads from the Eastern states terminate at Oakland these days, whereas just a single line sees fit to travel an extra 65 miles around the Bay to reach San Francisco. At the same time, the port of San Francisco has not served itself as well as it might have done in recent years. In particular, its authorities were slow to realize the potential of the container revolution that has transformed international shipping since the early 1960s; they took the view that this new method of handling cargo would not last, especially in any Pacific port. American shippers might have plenty of merchandise that could travel conveniently in big containers ranged along a freighter's deck, but what would the non-industrial nations across the ocean send back that could be safely packed in the same way? Coffee? You must be joking!

Brazilian coffee, however, has kept very well in those containers; and so has every other cargo, perishable or not, that sails the seven seas. Oakland did take the risk on containers and built the specialized facilities needed to handle them on the dock. She was lucky in that the federal government made a grant of $10 million when the capital outlay was required, because in the 1960s Oakland was a community with an unusually high level of poverty. Having built the facilities, Oakland was then astute enough to sign long-term contracts with the shippers, many of whom now seem to have moved permanently across the Bay. In one case, the move to Oakland happened because of San Francisco's sheer rotten luck: the city began building a special terminal for the benefit of the President Lines and was well along on the foundations when the whole thing was shaken apart by an earth tremor. The shippers, unwilling to face the consequent delay, decided to drop anchor in Oakland instead.

There is a feeling around the Embarcadero nowadays that the port of San Francisco is struggling uphill against mighty odds. True, by 1978 the port possessed six cranes capable of handling containers, whereas four years earlier there had been only one. True, also, that in the old Ferry Building the representatives of 30 nations have offices concerned mainly with trade. But the officials of the Port Authority seem to be pinning their hopes for a revival of San Francisco's international trade on some mighty slender possibilities. One of these is based on the assumption that ships will continue to be built larger and larger, with ever-deeper draughts. In which case, they say, we shall be in the driver's seat, with 40 feet of water alongside our piers, against poor old Oakland's 35 feet.

It is sad that a once-mighty port should have to contemplate its future in such terms. Perhaps the saddest thing of all is that San Francisco is clearly near the end of the road as a port of call for passenger liners. In 1978, both the *Monterey* and the *Mariposa*—U.S. ships that cruised the West Coast and the central and south Pacific—berthed here for the last time; never again, unless an international trend in transport is reversed, will a passenger liner sail under an American flag. Although the United States has dropped out of this declining competition, one or two nations still operate the cruising trade. But for how much longer?

When one of the remaining liners comes to the Bay and ties up at Pier 35 for a day or so, this end of San Francisco regains a little of its old verve. The taxi-cabs are waiting on the Embarcadero road to carry off the boatload of day trippers on their excursions around town. More often than not, sailing time is set for a minute to midnight and, in spite of the hour, San Francisco does its best to keep the old sentimental moment of parting alive.

As the taxis screech up with the last-minute gang, the folks who always almost miss the boat, a few score of friends—old and very new—are down at the pier, gazing up at the floodlit decks. The rails are lined with people looking down; and one or two of them throw coloured streamers to the watchers below. The specially employed Red Garter Band—a trumpet, a horn and a twanging ukelele—are on the pier too, mounted on a retired fire engine, knocking out "I Left My Heart in San Francisco", "Anchors Aweigh", "Yankee Doodle Dandy" and anything else that seems appropriate (the *Canberra's* passengers get "Rule Britannia" thrown in for good luck, and they're very welcome). The people on the pier jiggle from foot to foot in time with the music, and those up above swing their arms half a beat behind, while the crew prepare to haul up the gangway. Then, quite suddenly, someone notices that those towering steel sides have started to move, and cries of farewell begin to penetrate the honky-tonk sound of the band. Some people do shed a few tears. A couple of tugboats

Neon signs of sex shows and nightclubs flourish along Broadway, where a giddy variety of entertainments has attracted pleasure-seekers since the 1890s.

begin to butt and shove. A steward with his legs dangling out of a lifeboat five decks up calls "*Ciao, bambina*" to a girl weeping down below. Slowly, the great, beautiful, floodlit thing backs out into the night; and the musicians don't quit until she's well away from the pier—which is nice of them, a bit of San Francisco's generous charm.

The thing to do then, if you have a car, is to race that big liner to the Golden Gate, taking the steepness of Russian Hill in your stride while the ship is still straightening up to slide past Alcatraz. You cross the bridge, leave the car in a parking area on the far side and run back; and it's odds on that she will have slipped under the middle before you are 50 yards away. No matter. You will see her as a toy, where half an hour before she was a cliff. Her decks will be deserted now, though I can't think why; for even after midnight San Francisco is lovely from mid-stream. Another half hour and she is gone in a blaze of light, out into the Pacific beyond Point Lobos, bound for Honolulu or Sydney and eye-catching places in between.

As if to compensate for the creeping inertia that has beset the port, San Francisco (being American, and therefore passionately addicted to movement) decided in the 1950s to build an underground rail system that would transport a large proportion of the Bay population in and out of the city in the utmost comfort, and with enviable despatch. The Bay Area Rapid Transit system would become one of the modern wonders of the world, largely run by computers. Each train would have a human operator aboard, but most of his work would be done for him by a mishmash of wiring impressively contained within quite a small box. There would be 75 miles of track, spread like a swastika across the Bay area. Apart from anything else, this would be the largest underwater tube system on earth.

San Francisco grumbled a bit when construction workers started tearing up Market Street in 1967 to work on this marvel below the ground; but the workmen eventually filled in all the holes neatly and, in 1974, BART—as it is universally known—opened to the public. It is, indeed, a very striking creation. A ride on those cars is more comfortable than any I have known, except in Montreal and on London's modern Victoria Line; and it is quite as smooth and well-upholstered as either of those. The stations are a delight to a connoisseur of rail: spotlessly clean, glowing with soft light, making you want to run your hands over the marble texture of walls and benches. Only the subway in Moscow is in that sort of league. The subways of New York and Boston are antediluvian and grim compared with this.

Those Eastern systems do seem to work rather better than BART, though. So far short of expectation had the system fallen within four years of its start that the board of directors, in February 1978, declared a day of free rides throughout the 75 miles of track, as an act of contrition and a sop to angry commuters. Long before then, the local newspapers were campaigning against the system's inefficiency, and BART-baiting had become San Francisco's leading blood sport. BART officials had promised 90 to 105 trains operating every day, but the reality had become 33—when things were going well. They had vowed that trains would slide into stations between 90 seconds and two minutes apart, but the best achievement had been four to six minutes—and was usually a lot longer than that. People spoke of arriving at their destinations up to 45 minutes late; and the BART officials had to admit in the end that, if you were planning to travel their way, you'd do well to add three-quarters of an hour to your planning, or simply double the time written into the schedules. The public did not fail to remind them that BART had been launched behind the slogan "Pamper the Passenger." And here was the Assistant General Manager saying in cold print: "You can put any adjective you want on it from Lousy to Poor. But it's still Bad."

I'm sorry to say that I feel my heart leap at this failure of technology, for I never have thought much of machines over men. Bad luck for BART, of course, that some of its contractors never delivered the promised goods; but after a court battle, the Rapid Transit authority stood to collect $30 million in compensation for faulty equipment; few tears need be shed there. In any event, almost everything that could go wrong with machinery has gone wrong, so that on an average workday in the late 1970s more than half of BART's cars had to be pulled out of service. As for delays of cars that continued to run, sometimes they were caused by maladies as old-fashioned as rain falling on exposed sections of the track, an occurrence evidently unforeseen by the planners. Others happened because when one train broke down, it impeded another behind, there being no side tracks so that it could be shunted out of the way.

What maddened the commuters, on the receiving end of all this incompetence, was the language used to explain BART's failure to live up to its original ballyhoo. Nothing ever broke down because it was badly designed, stupidly planned or shabbily made. The failures came, it was usually said, from "impeded mode" or "down power" or "false presence" or some such obscuring language. But eventually the unhappy officials were driven to concede, in words everyone could understand, that behind most of BART's delays was "an antiquated 10-year-old computer".

The technological age needs no other epitaph—and San Francisco knows, more certainly than most places on earth, that once upon a time men founded things much better than this. Those cable cars are still running as promised a hundred years ago. And when they do break down, in their extreme old age, they have, like the city itself, a rich aesthetic of their own to see them through.

Sturdy Veterans of the Heights

In the evening rush hour, a Powell-Hyde cable car crosses the tracks on California Street, where the slots to the traction cables are visible in the central rails.

No remnant of San Francisco's cherished past has endured with such vigour as its fleet of quaint, toughly built cable cars. Inaugurated in 1873 to replace horse trams, the system uses 30- and 34-seat cars drawn by steel cables that move in channels 18 inches below street level. Cars on the three remaining lines—California, Powell-Mason and Powell-Hyde— still carry an average of 25,000 passengers every day over some of the steepest hills in the city, offering locals and visitors alike the fringe benefit of sudden dramatic views over the Golden Gate Bridge, the downtown districts, or the waters of the Bay. The cars have been protected under the City Charter since 1955 and acquired a unique status in 1964, when they were declared a National Historic Landmark in recognition of the place they hold in the hearts of modern San Franciscans.

Two cable cars ascend California Street while one descends. Maximum speed is set by the underground cables, which move at a constant nine miles an hour.

Pedestrians and vehicles mingle with cable cars on a busy section of Powell Street. Here, motorists may cross the tracks but must not drive along them.

Before oiling an underground pulley, a "trackman" checks it with a rod.

Known as "The Barn", the powerhouse of the cable-car system on Mason and Washington Streets uses 14-foot wheels to play out cables on the three routes.

At the controls, a driver, or "gripman", holds the lever with which he clamps the "grip" on the moving cable to start the car.

Geometrical markings and instructions painted in yellow along the tracks offer cues to the gripman. "Rope" refers to the cable.

Many stops and starts have ruined this gripman's leather glove, hanging on a control lever. The gloves, bought by the gripmen, can wear out in just a few weeks.

At the brick-paved terminus of the Powell Street lines, near Market Street (left), passengers and tourists watch a cable car being turned around for its next trip, back to Fisherman's Wharf. The turntable enables one man (above) to swing the six-ton car with relative ease. Only cars travelling the California Street route have driving controls at both ends and so do not have to be turned when they reach their destination.

4

A Singular Sense of Neighbourhood

One of the forms of restraint San Francisco has learned over the years is how to handle extreme wealth without the ostentation that characterized the beginnings of Nob Hill. Rich people are still entrenched up there, but they conduct themselves more quietly than they did in the age of railroad barons. The mansions of the Big Four were destroyed long ago, in the great earthquake of 1906. Nursemaids perambulate small children in a park where Collis Huntington's manor used to stand; Grace Cathedral rises on the site of the Crocker residence; Mark Hopkins' extravaganza has given way to a hotel that bears his name, with the additional title "Number One, Nob Hill" in stylish lettering over the front door; and where Leland Stanford stabled his horses, the University Club maintains a dignified silence about events within, having some years ago passed a resolution forbidding its officials to transmit the slightest information on club activities to the *hoi polloi* without.

The only Nob Hill dwelling to have survived the 1906 disaster—a brownstone built for James Flood, a mine-owner, who made $25 million out of Nevada's Comstock Lode—now houses the Pacific-Union Club. Far from being preposterously vulgar, the building would pass muster in Edinburgh at its most Calvinistically severe. Yet, with the exception of Grace Cathedral and a clutch of hilltop hotels, it is easily the most eye-catching structure in sight—Nob Hill these days running mostly to bland contemporary apartment buildings.

Modern equivalents of the vanished Nob Hill mansions may be found ranged along Pacific Heights, a hill a mile or so to the west. The residences there are discreetly opulent, with porticos and shutters, brickwork and stucco; they are insulated from the road by expanses of shrubbery and grass and, on at least one side, they have superb views of San Francisco Bay. They belong to the bankers and the lawyers and the businessmen of the city, and to those whose forebears invested wisely during the city's 19th-Century heyday.

Like Nob Hill residents, the inhabitants of Pacific Heights cherish their privacy from day to day, but they will throw open their houses once in a while to help advance the cause of some political candidate, for they are as prudent and calculating as the wealthy everywhere. On such occasions, visitors from the wider world may observe a would-be Senator or Governor questing for funds with a high likelihood of success. The guest-of-honour, whoever he may be, stands in a glow of attention and wields an ambidextrous smile. Behind him looms the cavernous stonework

Lovingly preserved Victorian homes in Alamo Square, in the Western Addition district, rise against a backdrop of modern skyscrapers, less than two miles away. San Franciscans pride themselves on a careful balance between the old and new, with tranquil neighbourhood rhythms providing welcome relief from the busier tempo of life in the downtown districts.

of his host's living-room fireplace. *Objets* from far-off lands are scattered around the room: an 18th-Century chest from Spain, a 17th-Century table from Bavaria and any number of odds and ends picked up on magpie flights across the world.

The host himself adopts a supporting role at such fund-raising events, dispensing opinions here, pressing a politically uncertain elbow there— his eyes flickering all the time to see who else has turned up, and to make sure that the aspiring politico is being plied with the guests who matter most. That is a bit difficult, with such a crush of people in the room that the Savonnerie carpet has almost vanished from view beneath their feet.

Another army occupies the dining room, ploughing its way through a very large tableful of dips, cold cuts, salad and fruit—all deployed around a three-foot-high model of City Hall moulded of ice. When the food is almost gone and City Hall's dome is beginning to drip, servants appear and whip the wreckage away. The guests take the hint; gradually there is an exodus across the front lawn to the street outside, and the house once again becomes a fastness, where discretion and decorum have the force of law.

Nob Hill and Pacific Heights represent one end of San Francisco's social and economic scale; at the other end is the Tenderloin, a district straddling the southern foot of Nob Hill. It is largely a ghetto of poor whites (only four per cent of its 20,000 people are black) and what makes it so deplorable is its proximity to so much wealth. Businessmen at the Hilton on the lower slopes of the hill are putting away the first dry martinis of the day only four blocks from a charity home where Franciscan friars have just finished dishing out a free meat-and-bean stew to 500 destitute old people.

In a number of places San Francisco falls short of its normal high standards of visual appeal, but only the Tenderloin is empty of the spirit that usually makes the city sing. True, a kind of robust life animates the sleazy streets of the district; but even here—in the porn shops, the "nude encounter parlours", the peep shows and the bars—the vitality seems to be spent on hope more than anything else. A girl sitting on a stool behind a window waves at men passing by; her eyes are too dull for her age, her cheeks too crudely crimsoned, and she looks as if she might be miming a puppet doll—but she has a different kind of earning power.

At least she has that. The most awful thing about the Tenderloin is the high proportion of its people who can hope to earn nothing at all, having failed at whatever it was that brought them to San Francisco in the first place. Many of them are old and inadequately fed. They are likely to inhabit single rooms in verminous flop houses, some of which are closed by City Hall from time to time because they are insupportably vile; other such places remain open because the authorities know that closing them will merely compound the misery they contain. Sometimes that misery becomes insupportable, too. The Golden Gate Bridge is not the only suicide spot in town. Once every 11 days, on average, someone kills

No. 1 Nob Hill—a vast, turreted mansion built in 1879 for railroad tycoon Mark Hopkins at a cost of $3 million—typified the uninhibited display of wealth in which San Francisco's first millionaires delighted. After the building's destruction in the quake of 1906, the Mark Hopkins Hotel—was erected on the site.

himself in the Tenderloin, and not all the suicides leave a note behind. It doesn't always matter whether anyone knows you have gone or not.

Mercifully, extremes of destitution and wealth are not typical of San Francisco. The norm of the city lies somewhere between the two. Indeed, San Francisco's greatest asset, apart from its physical beauty, is the basically even temper of its ways, which enlivens the heart of anyone fortunate enough to know it, and frequently bridges the gaps between social groups. This is a city with a good sense of balance in all things, with a feeling for community and with an appetite for the good life that, more often than not, most of its people manage to achieve.

The cohesiveness of San Francisco society is strikingly illustrated at the Opera House, just across the road from City Hall. Like many another edifice that arose from the ruins of 1906, the grey stone structure of the Opera House is a shade on the bleak side of architecture, resembling the People's Realism that the Soviet system has produced. But it is also the people's resort, whether mounting opera, ballet or symphony concerts. In every other opera-going city I have known, with the exception of Moscow, it is possible to predict which part of the house will be occupied by which socio-economic group; but such is not the case here. I recall being sandwiched, one night in the grand circle of San Francisco's Opera House, between two matrons swathed in fur and a young couple in jeans who entered with an infant carried across the father's shoulders in a backpack (and it was the music of Alban Berg, not the child, that caused the fur coats to abandon ship before the evening was out). The same social mixtures may be observed at the theatre, or when San Franciscans are eating out, or when—as they do a great deal of the time—they are enjoying the open air of the city's parks or the shores of San Francisco Bay.

A tangle of signs, wires, pipes and outmoded architectural ornaments festoons buildings along Eddy Street in the Tenderloin district, where tawdry flop houses and massage parlours flourish only a few blocks away from the discreet affluence of Nob Hill.

In most big cities, social groups tend to be pushed apart by the competitive rigours of metropolitan life, until they end up sniffing at each other like dogs on chance encounters. San Francisco is different because it is essentially a provincial place. It cannot claim leadership in any measureable way, except in having given birth to the largest bank in the world. Its music and its theatre are alive and well and good, but they are scarcely in the major leagues. Its newspapers are inadequate, relying too heavily on columnists of the most flatulent kind. But it offers other attractions. The city is small enough, with its population of less than three-quarters of a million, to function as a community; yet it is sufficiently diverse to have a great many neighbourhoods. In a country where the concept of the urban neighbourhood is often no more than a high ideal, San Francisco enjoys the real thing as a distinctive part of its everyday life, helped no doubt by the hills that split up the townscape and foster a sense of locality.

I cannot think of a more enviable urban existence than that enjoyed by the people who dwell on Telegraph Hill, which I pick out from other neighbourhoods merely because it's the one I know best. Except on rainy mornings, the custom there is to greet the day from the sun-deck of your house; and such is the configuration of the ground that you can observe your friends and neighbours on the descending rooftops below, having their breakfast, stretching themselves properly awake and making sure, as they survey their end of San Francisco Bay, that the Golden Gate Bridge still stands where it did the night before; or trying to judge from the clarity of the hills on the far side of the Golden Gate whether it would be wise to carry a raincoat or umbrella when setting off to work.

Gossip is the lifeblood of neighbours, and it flowed free and strong on the hill during my time there. We chatted with each other on the doorstep of the corner shop. We gathered around a tree that was blown down in a squall and wondered, conversationally, why City Hall hadn't yet sent workmen with chain saws since the damn thing had already been blocking our street for hours. We paused, in our slow ploddings up and down the hill, to exchange sharp comments about the fellow across the way who had lately felled three cypresses of his own and seriously perturbed the birdlife of our neighbourhood. It wasn't particularly exciting, all that neighbourly talk, but it linked us together.

And even though living on Telegraph Hill was like living in a village, the attractions downtown were never far away, so that our lives were balanced between calm and verve. In one direction from the hill, a stroll of 15 minutes or so would bring you to Fisherman's Wharf and its proliferation of eateries. In another direction lay the quieter pleasures of Washington Square, where people sit on benches around the grass, watch the comings and goings outside the Church of Sts. Peter and Paul, and observe the cable cars rattling along a stretch of level ground before the stiff haul up Mason Street on their way downtown.

A Legendary Fire Belle

By the middle of the 19th Century, no city in the world had greater need of a fire service than highly inflammable, robustly lawless San Francisco—and none had a more ardent volunteer than Lillie Hitchcock Coit, who is memorialized by a tower atop Telegraph Hill. Having been rescued from a hotel blaze in 1851 at the age of eight, she became the firemen's mascot, running beside the engines on every emergency call. Her wealthy parents sent her away to school, but separation from her beloved firemen only made her ill, so she was allowed to resume her hazardous, unofficial duties. She grew into a legendary figure, wearing a fireman's uniform, smoking cigars and staging boxing matches in hotel rooms. When she died at the age of 86, a throng of firemen turned out for the funeral, and she was cremated wearing the gold pin of Company No. 5.

Lillie Hitchcock Coit models her favourite attire.

Coit Tower's tip represents a fire-hose nozzle.

Coit Tower, paid for with the $100,000 Lillie Coit left in her will for the beautification of San Francisco, rises 170 feet above Telegraph Hill.

Or you could simply turn the corner of Chestnut Street, cross the flank of Telegraph Hill and potter down the North Beach section of Grant Avenue, where in the late 1950s the Beat Generation used to congregate. The street is now almost suburban in its quietly conforming ways. A succession of shops trade in what may be thought of as either antiques or junk (anything, that is, from old belt buckles to turn-of-the-century cribs); wisps of steam issue from laundries in between; and customers of an open-fronted restaurant toy with their wine and hamburgers, watching what's new in the human traffic of the street.

There are a dozen or so bars and eating places along this part of Grant Avenue, part of a San Franciscan gourmandizing heritage that is cherished as carefully as the cable cars. One place specializes in Italian family meals; and near the corner of Broadway is a genteel establishment where, when darkness comes, a lady in evening dress sings old-fashioned ballads to audiences sometimes numbering less than half a dozen, who sit among spotless tablecloths and an array of shining cutlery as rapt as if they were being given a command performance.

Turn that corner of Grant and Broadway and you find yourself in a neon-lit zone where foxy men invite you to step inside and see a strip show or variations thereon. ("Honeymooners get in free," they leer; and so they do, like everybody else, though they'd better have ten bucks ready for the first pair of obligatory drinks.) Or you can cross Broadway and descend along Grant into Chinatown, which is yet another world away from where, just 10 or 15 minutes before, you were gossiping with your neighbours in the peace and quiet of Telegraph Hill.

For San Francisco, this propinquity of neighbourhood and urban scene is not exceptional; only in their possession of a view across the most exciting stretch of the Bay are the inhabitants of Telegraph Hill better placed than most. And other neighbourhoods have exceptional views of their own. If you live in Sunset or Parkside, you may not see much of the Bay; but the Pacific itself is close at hand, rolling in breakers down the long straight line of Ocean Beach. If you live in Richmond, the honky-tonk of Broadway and the bustle of Chinatown are on the other side of the city (never very far in San Francisco); but you have at your doorstep the cosmopolitan life of Clement Street, which is Middle European in tone, with a Slavonic top register and a passage or two more commonly heard in the Orient. Above all, in the western half of the city, there is Golden Gate Park—an incomparable breathing space wedged between the densely populated ground of Richmond and Sunset.

Landscape gardening is a fine art at any time, but in the case of Golden Gate Park it has been nothing short of triumph over immense natural odds. Three years after work started in 1870, the *Santa Rosa Democrat* sneered at the nascent park as "a dreary waste of shifting sandhills where a blade of grass cannot be raised without four posts to support it and keep it from

Tradition-loving San Franciscans savour the ambience of 19th-Century opulence during Sunday brunch at the Sheraton Palace Hotel. The dining room, dating from 1909, is modelled on the covered courtyard of the original Palace Hotel, a $7 million edifice built in 1875 and described by its owner as "the world's grandest". It fell victim to the holocaust of 1906.

blowing away". Indeed, San Francisco's ambitious drea   of creating Arcadia-by-the-Pacific might have come to nothing if the Par   Commission had not recruited a young landscape gardener from Scotland, John McLaren, to take charge of the project in 1887. It was an inspired choice; Golden Gate Park became McLaren's life work, and he was still planting things in it not long before he died in 1943. In those early days, he painstakingly kept the sand from his precious grass by excavating each clump whenever the ocean wind threatened to smother it under dunes. He persuaded the city to sweep up the manure left behind by its horse-drawn traffic and dump it in the park to fertilize his plants. And when he had at last produced a healthy growth of sand grass, fescues and ryes, he magnificently insisted that not one square foot of his parkland should be polluted by notices warning visitors to "Keep off the Grass".

Golden Gate Park today has more than 1,000 acres where anybody may wander at will—an expanse that puts it among the great urban parks of the world (New York's Central Park runs to 840 acres, London's Hyde Park to 361). It contains plants and trees from every corner of the globe, as well as a stand of Californian redwoods, which McLaren started from seed in 1927 when he was 80, and which are already as tall as a house. And there is a great deal of wildlife besides. Buffalo and elk roam the park, and foxes that run wild are hunted to safeguard the waterfowl on the lakes.

The wealthy citizens of San Francisco have done much to make the park the remarkable pleasure ground it is today. One philanthropist built a museum and another housed a collection of Asiatic art in it. Additional benefactions provided for an aquarium and a hall of African exhibits. And even the rapacious Charles Crocker redeemed his name a little by coughing up the money to build a glasshouse modelled on the one at Kew Gardens near London. But these attractions merely begin the list. The park also has bandstands, baseball diamonds, horseshoe-pitching pits, a nine-hole golf course and a full-blown sports stadium that stages polo matches and football games in turn. You can study the heavens in a planetarium, or you can sip *lapsang* in an oriental tea garden, where you will be served by girls in native dress. There are very few things you can't do in Golden Gate Park, come to think of it, except drive your car along its 16 miles of roads on a Sunday, when traffic is banned so that San Francisco can enjoy its Arcadia in peace.

It is typical of this city that so much care and labour and wealth should have been expended on something that was created for pleasure. San Francisco has a gift for creating an enjoyable environment, and this talent finds expression in any number of ways, both planned and spontaneous. If I were to choose just one thing that characterizes the city's hedonist spirit, it would have to be the display of entertainments put on by its street performers, who are more numerous here than in any other Western city I have known. The performers are almost all young and have discovered

Victorian Miscellany

"Buildings that came to pass not by blueprint but by whim" is how one authority characterized the mixture of styles—Gothic, Italianate, classical or Georgian—seen in the façades of San Francisco's historic wooden houses. Generally known as Victorian, although they were built any time between the 1850s and the First World War, the houses reflect the exuberance and eclectic spirit of the earlier community.

On the front of one house (top row, near right), a Moorish horseshoe arch swells above a portico assembled from a hodge-podge of classical elements; on another, an art nouveau iron railing (middle row, centre) sets off heavy baroque brackets supporting an upper balcony. But the feature that has flourished and become most recognizably San Franciscan is the bay window (bottom row, centre and far right), an architectural device that allows in as much sunlight and warmth as possible in a city of fog and cool summers.

that they can make a better living by passing the hat around than by relying on an intermittent income from cabarets and clubs. Some of them reckon to take in $200 or more on a good weekend, but they are to be found in their accustomed places throughout the week as well. They stick, for the most part, to recognized spots. A fellow in British Army tartans daily makes the south side of Market Street stir like a clan-gathering to the sound of his bagpipes. Just across the way, where the cable cars reverse direction on a turntable, a woman in long skirts and shawl fills the air with wild Irish ballads. The "Bourbon Street Irregulars" work Geary and Stockton Streets with clarinet and saxaphone, drums, bass and guitar.

Most of the street entertainers are musicians of one sort or another, but if you make your way along Beach Street just north of Ghirardelli Square, you are likely to see a number of other talents in action. A juggler may be entertaining the line of people waiting at the terminus of the Powell-Hyde cable car. The spectators look a bit uncomfortable at first, but gradually they relax and start to grin in spite of themselves and, by the time the cable car arrives, they are fumbling for their small change without being asked. Nearby, Dr. Harry Lovecraft operates with the assistance of Eggbert, his white Java dove (the only bird I've ever seen stand on its head). Dr. Lovecraft is a magician disguised as a patent medicine man of the Old West and people nod in recognition as the patter begins to flow:

"What I'm really here for, friends, is not to sell you anything but purely as an advertising representative. If you suffer from any of the better-known aches and pains, if you suffer from high or low blood pressure, house-maid's knee or athlete's foot, then stay to listen to what I have to tell you, because when I tell you of some of the miracles that can be accomplished by a steady application of Dr. Lovecraft's magical medicines for mysterious maladies, you're going to say it sounds like magic. And that's exactly what it is." And while he is getting his breath back, he produces Eggbert from what he has just shown to be an immaculate and very empty white handkerchief.

From down the road we can hear the sound of a trumpet, which is doubtless at the lips of a popular San Franciscan named Grimes Poznikov; he styles himself the "Consultant to the Society for the Advancement of Non-Verbal Communication", but is better known in these parts as the Automatic Human Jukebox. Less visible than any other street performer, he spends his afternoons on Beach Street crammed inside a box resembling a Punch and Judy showcase. Notices on this box invite passers-by to select a tune from a long list and insert a coin through a hole; if a passer-by obliges, a flap will fall back, revealing Poznikov's face and trumpet for the space of a bar or two. When the *Wall Street Journal* canvassed foreign tourists some years ago about San Francisco's attractions, the Human Jukebox secured most of the votes.

Some of the outdoor entertainers of San Francisco have caught the eye of talent scouts and been launched into the big-time of U.S. show business.

As perfectly groomed as the model in the window, a young woman walks past one of the smart stores on Geary Street, a centre of cosmopolitan chic in San Francisco.

I have a feeling, though, that most of the performers would be loath to leave the streets, where they enjoy a lively rapport with their customers and can draw upon the passing scene to cultivate a relaxed atmosphere. I remember an occasion when a couple of motorists got into a heated argument within earshot of a juggler and his small attendant crowd. He observed them coolly for a moment, not pausing in his rotation of flaming torches through the air. Then he grinned slyly at his audience. "You couldn't enjoy that if you were sitting in the Opera House, now could you?" he suggested. Such is the carefree and amiable spirit in which San Francisco is particularly rich.

In an age when cities all over the world have been transformed by ferro-concrete in all its forms, and many historical townscapes have been obliterated almost before anyone realized it, San Franciscans have demonstrated a commendable obstinacy. They have refused to be dragged into the future by developers and planners. You have only to look around the city to appreciate the balance they have struck between old and new. If you go west across the broad artery of Van Ness Avenue, which was the great line of defence during the devastating fire of 1906, you discover a wealth of dwellings that have survived from the 19th Century.

Such houses can be found in lesser numbers elsewhere in the city, but they are the norm here rather than the exception. Any European with a sense of his own history can have a field day trying to spot architectural details that may have originated at any point between the boot of Italy and

Created in 1963 from an array of factory buildings up to a century old, the Ghirardelli Square complex of shops and cafés ranks as a masterpiece of renovation.

the top of the British Isles. One sees windows that Palladio first devised, frontages straight from Queen Anne's reign, turrets familiar to the royal incumbents of Balmoral Castle in Scotland; I have even noticed a gable on Vallejo Street that was first attempted in the helm spires of the Rhine.

All these houses are made of wood and are therefore painted overall— sometimes brightly, sometimes in drab, but almost always so as to catch and hold the eye. When I first saw them, it seemed to me that never before had I come across such a vast quantity of Victoriana (and it tickles me that these good republicans do refer to their "Victorian" buildings). Having been brought up among the remains of south Lancashire's part in the Industrial Revolution, close to Bolton and Manchester, I knew this impression to be an illusion—and eventually I realized why. What San Francisco has to show for its 19th Century is infinitely more attractive than those grimy brick buildings that surrounded me in my youth; all that Victoriana grabs the attention precisely because it has been so very carefully preserved.

In addition to cherishing their past, San Franciscans have been ready for battle whenever innovations threatened their amenities. One of the greatest triumphs of the preservationist impulse occurred in the late 1950s, when the entire city rebelled against freeways. At that time, freeway construction was in full swing throughout the United States, justified by politicians and contractors alike as the new epic venture on which all good Americans should be bound. Freeways, it was claimed, would stimulate travel and make commuting an exhilarating experience, allowing the suburb dweller to whizz around or over a city in minutes instead of the hours it could sometimes take.

The programme for San Francisco consisted of ten such marvels of communication, one of which was to continue north from the existing Bayshore Freeway, wind around San Francisco's corner of the Bay and tear off along the Embarcadero in the general direction of the Golden Gate Bridge. It was this Embarcadero Freeway that finally made the citizens revolt: the loop would have wrecked the foot of Telegraph Hill and mutilated the entire length of the city's waterfront.

The outcry was so general (though the State Highway Engineer later scoffed at "a very vociferous five per cent" and the mayor ruefully complained that freeways would be built to the moon before they had them in his bailiwick) that on January 26, 1959, construction of the monstrosity along the Embarcadero was halted when it was only one-third finished. At the same time, the city's Board of Supervisors voted to ban six of the nine other proposed freeways that would have despoiled the organic grace of the city with unlovely expanses of concrete on stilts.

Seven years later, a couple of the banned freeways (one of which would have traversed Golden Gate Park) again seemed likely to be built; and again the citizenry turned out at City Hall to cheer on the Supervisors to a six-five vote against the plan. To this day, the Embarcadero Freeway

A female mime artist with an appealing greasepaint grin carries her bag of stage props to the sidewalk venue where she performs regularly for passers-by.

Inside the world's most original jukebox, street entertainer Grimes Poznikov blows his trumpet in return for a passer-by's offering.

remains incomplete, its end hanging in mid-air near the old Ferry Building, with a steel barrier to stop the injudicious driver from taking off into space. The vestigial roadway, now known almost affectionately as The Stub, is a monument to what can be done against mighty odds when a community decides that it has had enough.

It is significant that San Francisco objected to freeways long before disenchantment with them became general throughout the United States. Other West Coast cities waited several more years before calling a halt to their own programmes; and not until 1970 did the *New York Times* pick up an echo of revolt among citizens in the East. As so often when it comes to guarding the quality of life, San Francisco showed the way.

These days, the preservationist spirit flourishes most successfully down at Ghirardelli Square, where Rapallo-born Domingo Ghirardelli set up his chocolate-and-spice business. He built his waterfront factories in brick and they have been cared for as meticulously as anything San Francisco has preserved in wood. For a time, however, the survival of this architectural legacy was in doubt. In the 1960s, the Ghirardelli business transferred to premises across the Bay in San Leandro and it seemed possible that the old buildings down by the water's edge might be razed to make room for apartments or high-rise offices. But a group of San Franciscans promptly bought the place and set a team of architects to giving it new life. Their imagination was so fertile and their ideas were so well executed by the contractors that in 1966 the American Institute of Architects struck (for only the second time in its history) a special medal for Collaborative Achievement.

What the architects have produced is a giddy assortment of shops and restaurants inside the old buildings, on a number of levels, with terraces and courtyards in between. You can pick and choose among toys, hammocks and oriental antiques in the Chocolate Building; you can ferret for clocks, Irish imports or swinging fashion in the Cocoa Building; you can rummage among jewellery, rugs and hobbies in the Mustard Building; and still you will have only trifled with a small part of the commerce that is here. If it were not for its elegant tone, this warren of tradesmen would bear a strong resemblance to the Grand Bazaar of Istanbul, with its ups and downs, its wayward corners concealing the next surprise and its vigilant shop-keepers attendant upon your slightest wish.

But the nicest thing of all is that the planners of Ghirardelli Square's brave new lease on life left as much of the 19th Century untouched as they could: a modish boutique is contained within walls of unfaced brick; seafood and wine is served beneath a ceiling supported by cast-iron pillars from the past. In the jargon of today, the transformed factories are a text-book example of recycled architecture—but their significance goes deeper. Ghirardelli Square, ingeniously balancing past and present, might stand as a symbol of San Francisco's gift for taking good care of itself.

A Unique, Thousand-acre Playground

Pirouetting like a ballet dancer, a youngster sails a frisbee across one of the verdant valleys created by park designer John McLaren from a wasteland of sand.

All cities have parks where nature is allowed to flourish and recreation facilities are at hand; but Golden Gate Park, extending three miles from the Pacific shore to San Francisco's centre, is unmatched for the variety of its delights. Within its 1,017 acres stand such attractions as a vast museum, a planetarium, an aquarium and a herd of buffalo. For those in search of sport, the choice ranges from a fly-casting pool to a polo field. But the real marvel of the park is its greenery—the work of a Scottish landscape gardener named John McLaren. Starting in 1887, he gathered thousands of plant species from all over the world, planted more than a million trees and created such prodigies of beauty on what had been sandy terrain that the city refused to let him retire; he remained park superintendent until his death at the age of 96 in 1943.

Flowers limn the Golden Gate Bridge and spell out a welcome outside the park's conservatory, built in 1879 as a gift from railroad magnate Charles Crocker.

Amid the tranquil pools, shady trees and exotic pagodas of the Japanese Garden, park visitors wander along bamboo-railed paths leading to an oriental tea-house.

A dolphin shows off for spectators in the Steinhart Aquarium. Donated by the millionaire financier Ignatz Steinhart in 1916, the aquarium has 208 fish tanks, ranging from five to 62,000 gallons in size. Dolphins and sea cows are among the most popular park attractions, along with a swamp area featuring alligators and deadly snakes.

At the park's nine-target archery field, two devotees take aim with compound bows, which allow the string tension to be adjusted according to strength and skill.

Cyclists on light racing machines follow the park's 7½ miles of cycle trails.

Three fitness buffs keep up a steady clip jogging towards the afternoon sun.

A suitably protected roller-skater speeds past a less energetic park-user.

Tennis pupils on one of the park's 21 courts form a chorus-line of forehands.

In the De Young Memorial Museum—named after newspaper publisher Michael de Young, who helped to found it in 1895—a park visitor pauses at a painting of the Annunciation by a 15th-Century Florentine master, before passing on to other Renaissance works. In addition to possessing a collection of European, Asian and American art unrivalled anywhere on the West Coast, the museum recounts the history of California through crafts and costumes.

Mexican folk dancers rest after a performance in the colonnaded Music Pavilion. On Sundays and holidays, the pavilion is the scene of free band concerts.

A girl muses beside the "Pool of Enchantment", near the park's museum.   A youngster lies full length for a closer view of the ducks on Mallard Lake.

A couple take their ease and enjoy the afternoon sunshine in an evergreen grove that is carpeted with daisies and adorned by a budding crimson fuchsia.

Responding to the call of the great outdoors, San Franciscans gather for a barbecue in one of the Golden Gate Park's glades. Barbecue pits are provided for the public at the north-east corner of the park, almost in the heart of the city.

5

The Tradition of Nonconformity

Ever since its earliest days, San Francisco has shown a remarkable tolerance of eccentrics and nonconformists. Innovations in attitudes and behaviour that would cause uproar in most other American cities are accepted here with hardly a murmur of disapproval. As a result, San Francisco is often said to be years ahead of the times—the place to go if you wish to see the lifestyle of the future.

Perhaps the most striking recent affirmation of its liberal outlook occurred in June, 1977, when observers calculated that at least 200,000 people marched through the city on what was proclaimed as "Gay Freedom Day", in support of homosexual rights. San Francisco had for some time been known as the gay capital of the United States, and the marchers' jubilation and contempt (there was a fair mixture of both) was directed at Dade County, Florida, and in particular at Miss Anita Bryant, a television personality who had once been a beauty queen and had recently led a successful Bible-thumping campaign in her home state to crush an ordinance that guaranteed equal employment rights to homosexuals. Miss Bryant supported the view that San Francisco had become a combination of Sodom and Gomorrah, and the enormous size of the gay march— equivalent to almost a third of the city's population—no doubt confirmed her in her opinion.

Belonging to a country that regarded homosexuality as a lawful condition some years before California got around to it, and having the greatest difficulty more often than not in distinguishing between a gay and a straight (particularly in San Francisco), I find it hard to get as excited as some about the city's latest great social phenomenon. I don't myself see how some people can estimate with as much authority as they do the number of homosexuals in the city, since no official census that I'm aware of yet takes account of our sexual tastes. Nevertheless, San Francisco's Human Rights Commission reckoned that at least half the people in the Gay Freedom March—or about 100,000—were self-proclaimed gays, while the rest were parents, friends, visitors and people who simply like to march in parades. The commission's calculation tallies with estimates from other sources that the number of gays living in San Francisco ranges from 90,000 to 120,000, or from just over 12 to nearly 17 per cent of the metropolitan population. Whatever the actual count, the gays have used the political muscle that derives from their numbers to make their presence felt, to a degree unequalled elsewhere in the United States. As early as 1972, the city council made it illegal for

Rising to her feet in an applauding crowd, a woman in outsize sunglasses signals her enthusiasm for the music at a jazz session in Stern Grove, a 35-acre park. Free concerts, attracting audiences of up to 25,000, are held during the summer in a natural amphitheatre surrounded by redwood and eucalyptus trees.

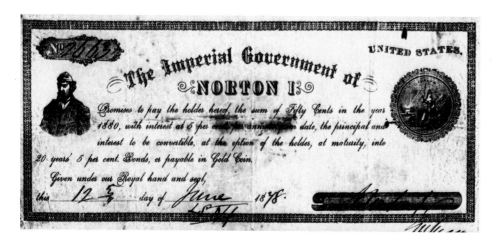

employers to refuse a job because of an applicant's sexual activities. And in 1976, one year before the Gay Freedom March, the Governor of California at last signed a bill that had been on the legislative docket for seven years. It was concerned with sexuality in general, but it became celebrated (or notorious) as a "bill of rights for homosexuals", who were thereafter to be allowed to do as they wished in private without fear of prosecution by the law. Victory came in the end only because the Lieutenant Governor, absent in Denver, flew home and was dramatically rushed from the airport in Sacramento, the state capital, to the Senate in order to break a voting tie. Since then, legislators from southern California have regularly called for repeal, but the gays in San Francisco have become an increasingly comfortable part of the city's life.

Within a few months of the gay march, a homosexual named Harvey Milk was elected to the city's Board of Supervisors. The San Francisco School Board passed a resolution implying that homosexuality would not henceforth be excluded from teachings about the facts of life; and the Police Chief announced that he'd be content to head a constabulary that included gays. He was even entertained at lunch, together with a dozen or so other officers, by the Polk Street Merchants' Association. It honoured him for conducting a blitz on all manner of lawless characters who had made Polk Street unsafe for both tradesfolk and their customers. The Mayor was present, too, and did not fail to suggest that other cities could do themselves a lot of good by looking towards this luncheon for a lead in exemplary civic behaviour. His enthusiastic gesture was not wholly disinterested. In San Francisco no citizen can hope to hold the office of Mayor for long without the support of the homosexual community.

This is not to say that everyone in town regards gays equably. There is a battalion of "cops for Christ" in the San Francisco Police Department who do not like the present trend. The Latins of the Mission District— close to the Noe Valley area where many gays live—are not enamoured of homosexual ways. Blacks may be heard complaining that they have been squeezed out of some residential areas by the subtle pressure of

Resplendent in a gold-braided uniform and plumed hat, the legendary San Francisco eccentric Joshua Abraham Norton (above) poses as the self-styled Emperor of the United States and Protector of Mexico. An English commodity trader, Norton had arrived in 1849 a rich man, but lost his fortune—and his reason— a decade later in a disastrous rice-market speculation. As "Emperor" he issued his own currency (one of his 50-cent bonds is reproduced above, left) and provided endless amusement to San Franciscans with his "royal" proclamations and advice to other world leaders. At his death in 1880, no less than 30,000 people attended his funeral.

superior homosexual wealth. Homosexuals themselves will concede that one reason why so many of the buildings they move into become show-pieces of careful restoration and thoughtful improvement is because, as one gay told me, "we have much greater disposable income than other people"—by which he meant that gays do not often have children. Still, no one can say that, in this way, they do not help to make San Francisco the attractive townscape that it is. Some people may think they vulgarize it from time to time. But it seems to me that the exhibitionist heterosexual couplings allowed at one well-known San Francisco bath house (its 35 "private" rooms have mirrors that can be transformed into windows, in case the occupants cannot function without an audience) are distinctly more off-putting than the lads walking arm in arm down Polk Street.

To much of the world outside San Francisco, all this may sound as if the city is toppling with moral decay. But San Francisco has never thought along lines like that. Its tolerance of every form of deviation from social norms stems from the days of the Gold Rush, when the town became especially rich in individuals determined to follow their own inclinations in the most startling way. Of these, none has been more celebrated than an Englishman named Joshua Abraham Norton. Arriving in San Francisco in 1849, he built up a prosperous shipping business on Montgomery Street. But in 1859 one of his ventures failed so disastrously that his sanity became affected. Thereafter, he became the outstanding character of the town, calling himself "Norton I, Emperor of the United States and Protector of Mexico" and dressing to suit the role in a gold-braided uniform and a plumed hat.

In this rig he regularly patrolled the streets, inspecting the police force on its various beats and berating the city fathers when their by-laws were not enforced. He corresponded with foreign heads of state, issued proclamations that the newspapers printed without a trace of ridicule, and even manufactured his own currency—which local tradesmen accepted without batting an eyelid, regarding his patronage almost as an honour. When Emperor Norton died in 1880, the entire town turned out for his funeral. Some time later the citizenry mounted another impressive wake for his dog Lazarus, who was killed by a fire engine.

Other eccentrics of the period included Frederick Coombs, self-styled professor of phrenology, who took to wandering the streets in powdered wig and full colonial dress as "George Washington the Second"; and a personage called Oofty Goofty (alias the Wild Man of Borneo), who decked himself in fur and feathers and enlivened the alleys of the Barbary Coast with strange animal cries. Oofty Goofty also invited San Franciscans to kick him for 10 cents, belabour him with a pool cue for a quarter, or clout him with a baseball bat for half a dollar. There were many such characters in the city that Oscar Wilde called the wickedest in the world, though I should have thought that the benevolent attitude adopted by San Francisco towards them said more for its rough-and-ready humanity than for its supposed sinfulness.

Given such an easy-going tradition, it is perhaps not surprising that San Francisco should have become the headquarters, more than half a century and two world wars later, of young people disenchanted by the state of Western civilization. In the 1950s, when the ideals of the struggle against Nazism had given way to the sterile bickering of the Cold War, San Francisco offered new inspiration as the home of the Beat Generation.

The seeds of the Beat Generation were sown, in fact, on the East Coast. Around 1944, Jack Kerouac and Allen Ginsberg—close friends and both aspiring writers—were studying literature at Columbia University. In New York they became acquainted with Neal Cassady, a natural anarchist and compulsive joyrider in stolen cars who was to be the model for Dean Moriarty in Kerouac's *On the Road*, and with William Burroughs, a Harvard graduate in anthropology whose apocalyptic view of society was to be elaborated in his novel *The Naked Lunch*. Burroughs was anti-establishment to the core and the underworld of drug addiction was already becoming his natural habitat. Both Kerouac and Ginsberg were much influenced by his views and it was they who then bore the Beat message across to the West Coast.

Kerouac became the father-figure of the Beats by giving the movement its name. A Beat, he reckoned, was someone who felt "a weariness with all the forms, all the conventions of the world. . . . So I guess you might say we're a *beat* generation." The Beats saw mankind as the increasingly depersonalized victim of science and ideology and believed that the only hope of salvation was for each individual to rediscover his own identity. The paths to self-revelation included alcohol, drugs, jazz, sex, Eastern mysticism—and if some of these pursuits also led to self-destruction, then so be it. The philosophy of the Beats was expressed most cogently by the novelist Norman Mailer, who stubbornly remained in the East. Writing when the Beat Generation was already thriving, he gave it a new name and declared that "the only Hip morality . . . is to do what one feels whenever and wherever it is possible, and—this is how the war of the Hip and the Square begins—to be engaged in one primal battle: to open the limits for oneself because that is one's need".

Another influential exponent of the Hip lifestyle was the poet Lawrence Ferlinghetti, who had abandoned New York for San Francisco "because it was the only place in the country where you could get decent wine cheap". Besides writing his own rebellious verse, he also established the City Lights Bookshop on Columbus Avenue, where the Beat literati regularly gathered to browse, read and talk. City Lights was claimed to be the first book store in America exclusively devoted to paperbacks. Certainly, it was a powerful outlet for the propaganda of the new culture.

The propaganda included an over-glamourized appreciation of the Hell's Angels, those speed-crazy, orgy-loving gangsters on motor bikes who began to terrorize California in the early 1960s. The Angels' leather-jacketed performances tended towards the suicidal, but to many of the Beats this seemed a marvellous way of living life while it lasted. The universal hero was the black (still labelled "the American Negro" in those days), seen by the Beats as a natural primitive who had suffered but had gained exuberance and comradeship, not to mention sexual prowess, in the process.

It is conceivable—just—that the message of the Beat Generation might not have spread beyond San Francisco if Ginsberg, self-publicist incarnate, had not stripped naked in 1955 to read his verse epic *Howl* at the Six Gallery, a converted garage on Fillmore Street. The work bristled with scatological references and was meant to be a howl of outrage against prevailing social mores. Kerouac, who ensured that the audience was liberally supplied with gallon jugs of California wine, has described that "mad night" in his novel *The Dharma Bums*: "Scores of people stood around in the darkened gallery straining to hear every word of the amazing poetry reading as I wandered from group to group, facing them and facing away from the stage, urging them to glug a slug from the jug, or wandered back and sat on the right of the stage giving out little wows and yesses of approval and even whole sentences of comment with nobody's invitation but in the general gaiety nobody's disapproval either. It was a great night."

As Ginsberg had intended, his poem drew much attention; and he was prosecuted for obscenity, though he eventually won his case. The poem also won the Beats their first national publicity, and before long the glad tidings were to be spread abroad—though some of us, I fear, took longer than others to give ear. As late as 1965, across the Atlantic in London's Royal Albert Hall, Ginsberg and Ferlinghetti appeared at a poetry festival that announced itself with the couplet:

England! awake! awake! awake!
Jerusalem thy Sister calls!

Jerusalem was at first located in the North Beach area of San Francisco, where Italians and other solidly conforming citizens had traditionally dwelt. Once the City Lights Bookshop was set up near the corner of Broadway, the acolytes of the new culture began to settle in the low rental property of the district. Insurrectionist coffee houses opened, bearing names like the Co-Existence Bagel Shop and The Place; and here the Beat Generation's message was passed on to any who would listen. Monday night at The Place was known as Blabbermouth Night, when crowds jammed its sawdusted floors and packed themselves within walls covered with local art, to hear speakers enlarge on whatever topic they chose, and to award a bottle of champagne to the orator who captured their fancy most.

Presently the streets of North Beach were thronged, almost 24 hours a day, by young people garbed in black turtleneck sweaters and jeans. They became a tourist attraction in their own right and, deciding to put the boot on the other foot, themselves hired a bus one evening to observe at close quarters the inhabitants of the Mark Hopkins and other expensive hotels, a gesture that was not much appreciated by the humourless patrons within.

In the early 1960s, however, the steady rise in North Beach rents caused Jerusalem to shift its ground across the city to Haight-Ashbury. Lying in the flatlands between the panhandle of Golden Gate Park and the northern slope of Mount Sutro, the Haight had been a middle-class area until the 1940s, when homeowners hurt by the Depression started converting their buildings into apartments to rent to factory workers producing armaments for the war effort. The new residents were mainly low-income whites, but soon after the war many of the blacks who came to San Francisco to labour in the shipyards at Hunter's Point and elsewhere around the Bay also started migrating into the Haight. It thus represented something of an ideal district for the Beats to colonize, though by the mid-1960s they were becoming emotionally separated from the blacks. Whites were preoccupied with the issues of Vietnam, while blacks resented the slow progress of the civil rights movement and tended henceforth to go their own way.

The Beat Generation did not abandon its old prophets, but it now found new ones who mostly preached revelation through drugs. One of them was the Harvard University psychologist Timothy Leary, who in 1960 had become very excited by his discovery of a black Mexican mushroom containing the hallucinogenic drug mescalin. Leary was less of a pioneer than he thought. He was unaware that the English novelist Aldous Huxley, long resident in California, had experimented with mescalin and another hallucinogen LSD (lysergic acid diethylamide), and in 1954 had published the results in his book *The Doors of Perception*; nor had he heard of Dr. Albert Hoffman's investigations into the effects of LSD, already well under way in Switzerland. Leary began a series of unorthodox experiments of his own at Harvard, insisting that both subject and experimenter should be drugged, that sessions should be conducted in sensuous surroundings and should be viewed more in a religious than a scientific light, and ended up being dismissed in 1963 for allegedly giving drugs to undergraduates. He went on to establish the League for Spiritual Discovery (L.S.D.) and appealed to the world to "turn on, tune in, drop out". San Francisco became his chosen stamping ground.

Another new messiah was Ken Kesey, sometime college wrestler, student of writing at Stanford, dabbler in drug experiments when he worked as an attendant in a psychiatric ward at Menlo Park Veterans Administration Hospital just down the Bay from San Francisco—and shortly to be celebrated as the author of *One Flew Over The Cuckoo's Nest*. Kesey held parties to tempt Ginsberg, Cassady and other influential Beats with what he promised were the truly fantastic effects of hallucinogens. He surrounded himself with a group of admirers called the Merry Pranksters (also known among themselves as Acid Heads) and at one stage bought a bus, painted it in Day-Glo colours, loaded it with drugs, placed Neal Cassady behind the wheel and toured the West Coast with Pranksters who helped distribute these wares *en route*.

San Francisco and its hinterland soon became notorious for Kesey's "acid tests": all-night carnivals marked by body-painting, psychedelic light-shows projected dizzyingly on the walls, over-amplified music belted out by local rock groups such as the Grateful Dead and Jefferson Airplane, and punch spiked with LSD, which was freely available to anyone with a thirst. In January, 1966, Kesey threw an epic party at the San Francisco Longshoremen's Hall that lasted for three days, was attended by no less than 10,000 people and ended with its chief sponsor having to get out of town fast to escape prosecution for possessing marijuana. (Incredibly, LSD was not then a forbidden drug, though it was to become so within a few months.) The media now began to wake up to the existence of the psychedelic movement and a new word was coined to describe the members of the rapidly growing colony in Haight-Ashbury. Norman Mailer had characterized the Beats of the 1950s as Hipsters. Their counterparts of the 1960s were to be known as "Hippies".

Haight Street was by this time becoming the headquarters of rebellious American youth. In the Psychedelic Shop, one of the Haight's chief attractions, Hippies could buy the papers needed for rolling cigarettes of pot, as well as psychedelic posters and the best-sellers of their generation: J. R. Tolkien's epic trilogy *Lord of the Rings*, Huxley's *The Doors of Perception*, and the impenetrable works of Marshall McLuhan, student

At a Hooker's Ball held in San Francisco's Civic Auditorium, a male wearing a gold catsuit and feather stole momentarily seizes attention with a solo dance.

A feathered mask and headscarf transform a face into a psychedelic vision.

Madcap Masquerade

Every October, San Francisco stages one of America's wildest and most outrageous fancy dress parties: the Hooker's Ball. Launched in 1974 by a feminist group named COYOTE (the acronym for Call Off Your Old Tired Ethics), the annual event has since become a highly successful fund-raiser for a host of women's causes, from the legalization of prostitution (thus inspiring the gala's name) to aid for battered wives and equal pay for equal jobs.

Attendance figures, starting at the 2,000 mark, consistently exceed 10,000—and the uninhibited vigour of the revels from year to year shows no sign of slackening. Throughout the night, men and women, gays and straights, flaunt regalia that range from bare-bottomed leather-and-chain outfits to topless bunny suits or seductive tiger-woman garb—a phantasmagoria of costumery that has provided an unexpected boost to the fund-raising efforts: many of the ball's patrons are there mainly to gawk.

of communications and inventor of the sentence "the medium is the message". To fuel their enthusiasm for new lifestyles, they could drop into the San Francisco Zen Buddhism Centre or the nearby Sexual Freedom League, which purveyed leaflets, medical advice and free propaganda.

Hippies in need could find succour at stores and soup kitchens opened in the area by a bunch of young radicals known as the Diggers; their name was derived from a group of 17th-Century English farmers who defied the laws of property in one of the earliest attempts at utopian communism. The food and other articles available in the establishments run by the Diggers were either scavenged or stolen. By the time they disbanded in 1968, the Diggers had plans to provide everything from free housing and legal advice to a free garage with mechanics who would show Hippies how to mend their cars.

The crowning manifestation of the Hip phenomenon took place on the polo fields of Golden Gate Park exactly 12 months after Kesey's 1966 marathon party: 20,000 people turned up to participate in "A Gathering of the Tribes for a Human Be-In". Most of the prophets were there to set the tone. Timothy Leary beamed benignly as thousands of LSD tablets circulated round the crowds. Ginsberg uttered a Buddhist prayer to start things off and gave his final benediction by blowing a conch shell as the sun set into the Pacific behind. Rock music was played, poems were read, life philosophies expounded. A young man descended by parachute. Hell's Angels guarded the sound equipment of the rock musicians, protecting it from other gentle folk participating in this general hullabaloo.

From the 1967 Be-In onwards, Haight-Ashbury and all it represented in the popular esteem of the day descended from mindless enthusiasm to sordid self-destruction. What happened at Golden Gate Park between Ginsberg's prayer and his solo on the conch shell was heard as a clarion call across the United States and far beyond, much more impelling than any of the propaganda that had been put out before. Armies of youth began to roll up to the Haight to share the satisfactions of a so-called Summer of Love. They found all manner of tradesmen waiting to rip them off—mostly with drugs, not all of which were pure. The kids progressed from hallucinogens, to barbiturates and later still to opiates. Soon they were destitute and sick, dependent on the voluntary efforts of well-wishers, particularly the doctors who set up and ran the Haight-Ashbury Free Medical Clinic on Clayton Street.

According to one of those doctors, San Francisco was at the time faced with its most serious medical emergency since the 1906 earthquake and fire. It was not simply that kids were going blind or off their heads with adulterated drugs. The overcrowding that occurred in the Haight also played its part in spreading every imaginable infection, including measles, mumps, influenza, pneumonia, dysentery, typhoid, meningitis, plague, tuberculosis, venereal disease and hepatitis. People also turned up at the clinic seeking treatment for the most awful wounds, caused by treading barefoot on broken glass and later on excrement, having been unaware of anything on the sidewalk because they were stoned out of their minds. Rival gangs began to rampage and smash up the place until, as one witness said, Haight-Ashbury looked like Berlin at the end of the Second World War. Tourists, who had earlier visited North Beach to inspect the animals in the human zoo, now took their evening drives to peer at the happenings in the Haight.

The Summer of Love was finished and, to many of the participants, so was the Hippie ideal itself. Members of the Haight community gathered in Buena Vista Park that autumn to mourn the Death of Hip with a funeral ceremony and Hare Krishna chants. But the circus of horror was by no means over. In the first two months of 1969 alone, 17 murders, 58 rapes, 209 cases of assault and some 1,500 burglaries were reported in Haight-Ashbury. At a summer rock concert held on a speedway track at Altamont, across the Bay, the Hell's Angels were offered $500-worth of beer by the management of the Rolling Stones to protect the rock group from their fans. Every mind-blowing drug known to civilization awaited the kids who turned up. One gang of pushers from Berkeley distributed more than 5,000 tablets of adulterated acid in a few hours. Eventually the Angels, wielding weighted pool cues, went wild and four people died in the ensuing violence. A young black was stabbed to death just below the stage on which the Rolling Stones were singing *Sympathy for the Devil*.

By then thousands who had followed the prophets were in hospitals or behind bars. The cult murderer Charles Manson, once a patient at the Free Clinic, was leading his amazons into orgies of appalling slaughter in Los Angeles. The prophets themselves were dispersed, having long since washed their hands of the dreadful mess they had inspired. Mailer was still preaching from afar; but Neal Cassady, the "burning, frightful, shuddering angel" of Kerouac's *On the Road*, had died in Mexico while under the influence of drugs and alcohol. Kerouac himself was in Florida dying of liver damage. Leary, who was facing a prison sentence for possessing pot, had become a martyr. Kesey, who had also run foul of the law for possessing pot, was waiting out a three-year probation order on his brother's farm in Oregon. Ginsberg was in New York recovering from a motor accident.

One noble thing to emerge from the wreckage was the devoted work of unpaid people who laboured in the Haight-Ashbury Free Medical Clinic, trying to heal the endless procession of broken bodies and minds. Although the San Francisco medical profession as a whole preferred not to soil its hands with sickness that couldn't be paid for, a handful of doctors dedicated themselves to the project. They were supported by a growing number of social workers and untrained volunteers. Another heartening result of the psychedelic disaster was the large number of kids who first turned to the clinic for aid, later worked there to succour others like

The grim silhouette of Alcatraz Island dominates the Bay. Closed in 1963 as a cost-saving measure, the former federal prison is now a tourist attraction.

themselves, and eventually decided to go through medical school and emulate the real heroes of the Haight. The rock musicians helped keep the clinic going by giving concerts to provide it with necessary funds. But there wasn't much else to applaud in San Francisco then.

What happened in Haight-Ashbury was, from start to finish, a case of high idealism becoming corrupted by stupidity, ignorance and greed. And it is entirely consistent with the history of San Francisco that idealism was not quenched by the trauma of the immediate past. As the new decade began, drugs became bad news, and ecology—sweet and wholesome thing— began to rival the Vietnam War as Local Topic No. 1, thereby doubtless saving the sanity of the next wave of youth that might have rushed like lemmings for the old Haight.

In 1973, however, the Bay area was shaken by another event that sprang, in a grotesque way, from the corruption of high West Coast ideals. This was the kidnapping by the Symbionese Liberation Army of the California newspaper heiress Miss Patty Hearst. It was ludicrous of Miss Hearst's abductors to call themselves an army, for there were never more than a score or so who carried guns. They were notable, more than anything else, for their curious taste in adopted names. Their leader, a petty hood whose real name was Donald DeFreeze, called himself General Field Marshal Cinque. He was black, but his soldiers were (like most of the cannon fodder expended on the Haight) white upper-middle-class dropouts. Second in command was General Teko, the alias of William Taylor Harris, a veteran of Vietnam, with a master's degree in urban education.

I don't think it can be contested that this motley crew were motivated by social ideals, even though these found their expression in homicidal and other lunatic forms. The SLA slogan was: "Death to the fascist insect that preys upon the life of the people." Their most imaginative act was not so much abducting Patty Hearst from her Berkeley apartment and renaming her Tania, but the "good faith" gesture they demanded of her rich and frantic parents. The Hearst family was invited to distribute vast quantities of foodstuffs, free, to the poor people of the Bay area; and you can't be much more idealistic than that.

What followed, however, was a bloody shambles. The Hearsts did distribute $2 million-worth of food—indeed, they were prepared to spend twice as much again to have their daughter back—but there was a riot in Oakland when 13,000 people jostled and fought to get near the trucks from which food packages were being handed out. A woman lost an eye when a rock came through her car window and she sued the Hearsts, the City of Oakland and the "People in Need Charity"—which organized the distribution—for $1 million.

In San Francisco a couple of weeks later, the Hibernia Bank was robbed, and Patty Hearst herself, armed with a gun, was identified on closed-

Browsers linger over the offerings of the City Lights Bookshop, open seven days a week. Founded on Columbus Avenue in 1953 by the poet Lawrence Ferlinghetti, City Lights became famous as a gathering place for such Beat Generation writers as Jack Kerouac and Allen Ginsberg and was the first bookshop in the U.S. to carry paperbacks only. It has remained in the literary swim by continuing to publish the works of little-known West Coast poets under its own City Lights imprint.

circuit television as one of the raiders. The end of the SLA came within two years of its mobilization, when the leaders were besieged by police in a flaming cottage in Los Angeles and killed in a shoot-out under the lenses of television cameras, almost within sight and sound of Hollywood. There followed an interminable saga in the courts, to determine what precisely had become of Miss Hearst's mentality between her abduction in 1974 and her appearance as an active member of the SLA 18 months later. All these events received a disproportionate amount of attention because they involved an heiress. The only real significance of the SLA lay in its origins, and what it thought it was trying to do, and the fact that it emerged when and where it did. It was nonconformity gone mad, and one might argue that it couldn't have happened anywhere else.

San Francisco will doubtless surrender itself one day to yet another social phenomenon still undreamt of, for this city seems forever to be in search of renewal. A fond inhabitant with a vivid turn of phrase described the place to me as like "a restless whore, always looking for something fresh". Still, the city has quietened down considerably since those years of tumult that followed the Beats and the Hippies. The Haight has been restored again to a civilized neighbourhood, where middle-class professionals abide amicably alongside very quietly nonconforming youth.

The Free Clinic functions as splendidly as before, treating the poor and the indigent of the town. Its various treatment centres are spread around the Haight and deal with some 50,000 patient-visits a year. But no longer are there lines of emaciated Hippies patiently waiting their turn to pass through the door of the clinic on Clayton Street; and alcoholism has become one of the biggest problems they tackle. Elsewhere in the city and around the Bay, cocaine addiction has risen steadily, but it has become almost wholly the province of the well-to-do, who alone can afford the exorbitant cost. In the Haight, happily, addiction to hard drugs has, for some time now, been declining. No one is nervous any more about using pot. Possession of small amounts of marijuana was decriminalized in California in 1976 and the worst punishment that you are liable to incur is to be fined a modest $100.

Men of letters still flourish in the city, though nowadays they create little more than a local stir. The writers of renown associated with San Francisco have always tended to be birds of passage even when, like Jack London, they have had their origins on the Bay. Usually they dropped by, filled their notebooks with the material they sought, and sheered off again to more profitable or more sympathetic base camps in the East or even farther afield in Europe.

Just once, during the age of the Beats, San Francisco inspired a literary fashion that deeply influenced American youth (and not only them) in the first genuinely popular movement of its kind since Ernest Hemingway, F. Scott Fitzgerald and other writers emerged in the 1920s to speak for the "Lost Generation". Probably because the recollection of those stirring Kerouac years remains fresh, there has been ever since something slightly forlorn about the writing trade in San Francisco, as though a vigorous tide had turned leaving only damp sand upon the beach.

All the big publishing houses have their headquarters in New York or elsewhere in the East, and the attention paid to book reviewing by the local press is laughable when compared with the industry of the *New York Times* or even the serious application of the *Washington Post.* Such rivalry as exists between New York and San Francisco is nowhere more pronounced than in the writing trade, and the scribblers of Manhattan can be very patronizing about their fellow-craftsmen in the West, whose life, they are wont to say, is too flabby to produce tough, creative art.

The penmen around the Bay usually shrug at such insults, go out and take a stroll, enjoy the splendid view from the top of the street, and thank God they haven't had to step over piles of uncollected garbage on the way. Tomorrow morning they will do a little more work on the opus that may keep them sublimely afloat. Once in a while, however, they can be discovered indulging in a bit of retaliation. During my last visit, a catalogue of new books that was issued from the presses of City Lights (which publishes as well as sells) included a volume of verse by Stefan Brecht with the following observation: "This collection by the New York critic, philosopher and late-night actor (generally ignored by New York publishers) is a literary discovery of the first order." Although I don't imagine the book sold more than a few hundred copies along the Coast, poets have never lacked a small audience here; just as importantly, they have never been short of small publishing houses whose lack of heavy overheads allows them to cope with slim poetic works. It is the men who write 30,000 words or more who have to look East if they are to see their names in print.

City Lights has remained a focal point for the city's *avant-garde*. You may see, browsing among the shelves, bored-looking matrons who have been taken on a pilgrimage by husbands trying to recapture the essence of their salad days. They will, I suspect, find that something has changed since the decade when they set the world on edge with their carefree noise. The old prophets are still venerated here and Ginsberg has long since been canonized. The once outrageously subversive *Howl* is heading for its 30th printing, with more than 300,000 copies released around the world—in itself a hallmark of respectability as these things go.

The new nonconformists are nurtured as the old once were, but I imagine that, when the works of the Beat Generation first landed on the shelves, they did so with much more of an echoing thud. Any homosexual, for example, who has come to San Francisco with the feeling that this is where the world has been set on fire must be rather disappointed to find that at City Lights—of all book stores in town—*Gay Source (A Catalog for Men)* is sandwiched between *The Compleat Angler* and a coffee-table tome on Pennsylvania Dutch Folk Art. You can even buy City Lights tee-shirts at the counter, the ultimate symbol of young American conformity.

Some nonconformities, however, never change in this place. Sit at your sidewalk table a few hundred yards from City Lights' flickering beacon and you may spot—amidst the winking, knowing, leering neon lights of Broadway—the heir to Emperor Norton. His name is Peter and he hails from Maine, and somewhere along the line the bottom fell out of his life. He patrols North Beach with his Dalmatian dog always at his heels and in the evening he generally stops outside Enrico's café. Here he coaxes his Dalmatian very carefully into a cardboard box and tucks the animal up with newspapers so that it won't catch cold. The dog rests its head on the edge of the box and watches patiently as its master shuffles away on some errand across the street.

Presently Peter returns, a rather bent figure in clothes that have seen much better days, but a man with a face of which a patriarch would be proud. He has lost no dignity; when he cadges a cigarette and joins you in a drink, it is still a matter of man to man. He calls you "Sir" in the old-fashioned American way that has never been stained by the inferior usage of the English; it is a token of self-respect as much as an acknowledgement of his respect for you. He is also very gracious to the woman at your side, though there is an old Adam inside who would dearly like to flirt. Enrico's, which will roughly bounce a drunk, accepts Peter for what he is. I hope they make sure that San Francisco one day salutes him the way it knows how, and thinks to take care of his dog when he has gone.

Easy-going Lifestyles

Finding peace and tranquillity in his local laundromat, a bearded customer settles himself in the lotus position and waits patiently for his wash to be ready.

According to a foreign observer of the contemporary Californian scene: "It is as if, after centuries of being cooped in school, the American people have here burst yelling into the playground." In unconstrained San Francisco, freedom takes many forms. The visible freedoms of Hippiedom still continue, from beards and long hair to beads and sandals. Casual dress, or very little dress at all, serve as reminders that San Francisco was the first to give the world both jeans and "topless" nightclub dancers. But even the conventionally inclined make their own subtler responses to the city's liberating magic, moderating their stride to a more leisurely pace, speaking with a soft timbre, emphasizing a commitment to take life as it comes. In the evocative words of a 1960s pop song about San Francisco, they wear—metaphorically at least—flowers in their hair.

Under a brashly explicit sign, two girls, a baby and a Great Dane survey Broadway's nightclubs, where the "topless" fashion was born in 1964.

In a city where almost anything goes, a girl does her own thing in style—wearing a slinky evening gown in the full glare of the midday sun.

A street artist who favours an unconventional form of transport pauses to show samples of his work to a diner emerging from a restaurant.

A well-dressed visitor to the grounds of the Palace of Fine Arts, built on the edge of the Presidio in 1915 and now a museum, makes friends with the blackbirds.

A motor-cyclist, sun-reddened from long rides through the California countryside, negotiates heavy traffic as he comes up Broadway for a night on the town.

Bundled up against the wind, an elderly San Franciscan pauses on O'Farrell Street in a coat and hat that seem to belong to another age and another climate.

Face to face in the California melting pot, a blond child takes a long, wondering look at an exotic stranger. As one perceptive observer wrote more than a century ago: "San Francisco is a city where people are never more abroad than when they are at home."

6

A Rich Racial Mix

San Francisco has one of the richest racial mixes in the world. At the time of the last census more than 45 per cent of the population had either been born outside the United States or were the first generation of their families to be reared entirely on American soil. Even in the polyglot U.S. this is a very high proportion indeed—of the 50 largest American cities only Miami surpasses it—and it accounts for a great deal of the colourful spirit exuded by the city on the Bay. San Francisco may never have offered the same economic prizes as New York, which has always represented the jackpot for immigrants seeking their fortunes in the New World; but there have been other advantages to compensate.

The most obvious mark of San Francisco's cosmopolitan character is noticeable the moment you consider where your next meal is coming from. If you're planning to eat at home and need to go out to buy the food, the chances are high that within half a mile you will find shops not only selling every vegetable California's farmers can produce (almost every vegetable, that is, known to man; the Polynesian *kumara* is the only one that I myself have not yet succeeded in tracking down) but also offering every exotic preparation of meat. There is an establishment in North Beach (and I don't suppose it's the only one) where a connoisseur of sausages can pick and choose among varieties that have originated in half a dozen different parts of Europe: *schinkenplockwurst* from Germany, *mortadella* from Italy, *saucisson* from France, *gyulai* from Hungary, *kabanos* from Poland and *loukanika* from Greece.

As for eating out, the choice of foreign restaurants in San Francisco and around its Bay is bewildering to anyone congenitally incapable of making up his mind. Plenty of cities offer a wide variety of foreign cuisine, but I don't know of any other where subtle distinctions are so carefully maintained. One restaurant is dedicated to the cooking of Afghanistan alone, which is about as recondite as you can get in these matters. There are at least five places catering to those whose digestive juices are most stimulated by Basque cooking. The man who likes to eat the Central- or South-American way can happily progress on successive nights, in different places, from ground beef tongue fried with sweet bananas (from Nicaragua) to pig's feet in batter (El Salvador) to corn dough stuffed with chicken (Peru). What's more, the owners of such establishments are not simply content to serve you with their traditional food; they go to considerable lengths to reproduce a proper atmosphere. At a restaurant on Union Street, an Englishman may tuck into roast beef or steak-and-kidney

Tossing the head of a ceremonial dragon, the first of the 50 dancers who carry the 150-foot-long beast leads the traditional Chinese New Year parade down Grant Avenue, the main thoroughfare in Chinatown. San Francisco's 70,000 Chinese—the most colourful and tightly knit minority group in the polyglot city—form the largest Chinese community outside Asia.

pudding beneath pictures of several celebrated cricket teams—photographs that have long since been collectors' items back home.

No less revealing of San Francisco's cosmopolitan nature is the published fare being sold on the news-stands. Around this city, you will see papers and periodicals for readers of almost every race. They will not be flown in from abroad (unlike American cities in the East, San Francisco does not pay much attention to the foreign press), but have been produced in the United States, very often in the city itself. Some of these publications are in English, like the Japanese newspaper whose title *Hokubei Mainichi*, meaning *North American Daily*, is the only concession to the native language of its readers. Others, such as *L'Eco D'Italia, Neue Zeitung* and *Le Californien*, are presented in foreign tongues. The Filipinos have four newspapers of their own circulating around northern California, and the Chinese enjoy four dailies and eight different weeklies in oriental characters. All these publications tell what is happening within the different ethnic groups. But even more, they enable immigrants to keep in touch with events in the old country. Thanks to overseas coverage, there won't be many soccer-loving Italians in San Francisco who can't tell you what happened the other week when Juventus met Milan.

The same could doubtless be said of Italians living in New York, though people with strong racial or national ties do not always react in the same fashion on both sides of the United States. The Jewish community of San Francisco, while substantial, is not as much a political force as in New York, nor is it nearly as strident in its support of Israel's cause. The Irish, on the other hand, seem to be more vigorous these days than their brethren in the East; they remain strongly committed to the Provisional IRA view of the happenings in Ulster in recent years, a version of events that no longer gets universal sympathy from Irish-American politicians in the East.

The Irish form a decent segment of society in San Francisco, as they do in practically any city of the United States; but on one count at least, their cultural influence has been disproportionate. There are times when I am ready to believe that Irish coffee is the city's favourite drink. A tavern on Beach Street actually claims to have invented the blessed stuff a couple of decades ago—and Irish coffee is the main standby during intermissions at the Opera House.

San Francisco is generally much more mindful of its connections further west, across the Pacific. This westward orientation is reflected in school notices to parents, which are issued in five languages: English, Spanish, Chinese, Japanese and Tagalog—the national language of the Philippine Islands. People have been migrating here from the Philippines since the 1920s. Although most of the early arrivals provided labour for farms throughout the state of California, Filipinos nowadays are spread as widely through San Francisco's work-force as any other group.

Shadowed by his bodyguard, a silk-clad merchant strides through old Chinatown in a turn-of-the-century view by Arnold Genthe, who compiled the only photographic record of the district before its destruction in the 1906 earthquake and fire. Although merchants and businessmen enjoyed only modest social status in China, they became the leaders of the expatriate Chinese in San Francisco and were regarded as the mandarins of the New World.

On arrival they have consistently dropped anchor in the Mission District, where the majority of San Francisco's Latins abide. (The Philippine Islands were long part of Spain's empire, and Spanish is widely spoken there.) Typically, when they have found their feet, they have moved out to the south-western end of the BART line, in Daly City. There, the newcomers gradually adjust to the American way of life, acquiring outlooks that they never had before (there is no word in Tagalog, for example, denoting guilt or shame), adapting their extended family system to the more rigid social structures of Western culture, and accustoming themselves to a diet that includes such previously unknown staples as bread and potatoes. There are 115 Filipino clubs and societies in San Francisco to help the process of amalgamation along. But amalgamation goes only so far: despite laws against cock-fighting—a favourite Filipino diversion—the blood sport is still staged in a number of discreet places around San Francisco Bay when the police aren't looking.

The Japanese are deeply rooted in San Francisco now, having emerged from the upheaval caused by the Second World War. They originally came to California in the 19th Century to work as agricultural labourers and domestics and to supplement the labour force that the railroad barons had imported from China. As with the Chinese, discrimination against them was rife, and it lasted even longer. Until 1952, no Japanese born outside the United States was allowed to become an American citizen—a ban that, by then, applied to no other immigrant group.

Conceivably this prohibition would have been lifted a decade earlier if Pearl Harbor had not been attacked; but in the hysteria that followed America's entry into the war, things went sorely for the Japanese who had lived respectably in San Francisco all their lives. On February 19, 1942, President Franklin D. Roosevelt signed the infamous Executive Order 9066: all Japanese on the West Coast were ejected from their homes, often with no more than 48 hours' notice. They were allowed to take with them only those possessions they could carry by hand, and Americans of British, German, Italian or any other extraction picked up their hastily sold property for a song. Some 117,000 Japanese were herded together in a number of internment camps in the desert mountains above Death Valley, close to California's eastern border, and elsewhere farther east. Presumably the locations were chosen because the inmates would be too far from the coastline to flash signals to roving enemy submarines.

When the first internees were released at the beginning of 1945, many were without homes and found hotel rooms hard to obtain because of the proprietors' hostility. Some who, instead of selling their homes had let them to tenants three years before, returned to find that locked rooms had been broken into and personal possessions stored there had been stolen or damaged. Cars had disappeared or had been stripped. Some businessmen were unable to re-enter their old firms or failed to get licences to start new

The folded wrap and elaborately flowered coiffure of a Filipino woman add an exotic tone to the early morning bustle on California Street. San Francisco's Filipinos tend to find assimilation less of a problem than do the other Asian minorities; 25,000 strong, they are spread throughout the city.

Their heads decorously covered in pale blue mantillas, women of San Francisco's Italian community (left) listen in front of a dais at Fisherman's Wharf as a priest celebrates the annual Blessing of the Fleet, a ritual introduced to the New World by Sicilian fisherfolk. Held on the first Sunday in October, the ceremony begins and ends with prayers at Sts. Peter and Paul—the mock-Gothic church (right) that serves as the spiritual centre of North Beach.

ones. By the summer of 1945 much of the anti-Japanese feeling had subsided, and accommodation and jobs became easier to obtain, but the Hagiwara family who for three generations had managed the Japanese Tea Garden in Golden Gate Park never did regain their concession, and many Japanese who had been well-to-do before the war ended up doing menial jobs in industry or domestic service.

If there is still bitterness at this long and rather shabby persecution, the Japanese-Americans conceal it well, although when the older ones meet each other for the first time they usually ask the same question: "Which camp were you at?" Like every other distinctive group, they dwell in every part of the city now, but they also have their own Japanese Town on the edge of the Western Addition, so-called because it was settled after the downtown area and the hillsides of the waterfront had been built up. Japanese Town does not look very different from any other part of the city as far as the buildings go. But in their windows and in their small garden plots, the inhabitants sometimes give their origins away, with a bonsai tree here or a paper lantern there. Every year a magnificent cherry blossom festival is held and, on midsummer's day (*Obon* to the Japanese), girls clad in kimonos go dancing through the streets.

A much larger minority in the city are the Chinese, who are more than 70,000 strong today. The Chinese are in every job and profession, but they are especially active in real estate: it is estimated that, although they make up less than 10 per cent of the city's population, they own 20 per cent of the property. Much of it stands in Chinatown, an area of 24 blocks spread around the middle section of Grant Avenue. The Chinese know this thoroughfare as Du Pon Gai—their version of Dupont Street, which was Grant's name before the 1906 earthquake. To the north, Columbus Avenue and Broadway form Chinatown's border with Little Italy, where pasta comes in every form in the restaurants, and where men bowl the

wooden balls of *bocce* along a dirt court near Washington Square. To the south, Chinatown becomes downtown San Francisco at Bush Street. To the east, the district ends at Kearny Street; to the west, at Mason Street. Within these boundaries, Chinatown is a world apart. There is nothing to match it in size or atmosphere outside the Orient itself.

To understand this, it is necessary to appreciate the circumstances that brought the Chinese to San Francisco in such huge numbers. Most ethnic groups arrived individually or in families, in one boat after another, over a long period of time; but the Chinese arrived early and in droves. They were mainly from the south China coastal province of Kwangtung, a heavily populated area cut off by mountains from central China and traditionally outward-looking. Its chief city, Canton, had been the only Chinese port to have much contact with the Western world before the mid-19th Century. Between 1839 and 1842, trade and agriculture in Kwangtung were disrupted by the Opium War, fought between the British and the Chinese and concentrated in the area around Canton; later, the province was hard hit by the Taiping Rebellion, which broke out in 1850 and brought anarchy and famine to many parts of the Manchu Empire before the fighting ended 14 years later. For the people of Kwangtung, San Francisco and the bustle of the California goldfields offered an escape.

The first known arrivals were two men and a woman who came in the clipper *Eagle* in 1848; but by the end of 1852, with the Gold Rush well under way, 18,000 Chinese had reached San Francisco. A man named Wah Lee had established the first Chinese laundry in town, and within 20 years there would be 2,000 of his compatriots engaged in the same trade.

From the start, the Chinese faced racial antagonism from the settlers of European descent, and this encouraged them to congregate in the ghetto that soon became known as Chinatown. At first, one of the chief rabble-rousers against Chinese immigration was the railroad baron Leland Stanford; but he soon changed his views when his colleague Charles Crocker pointed out the advantages of cheap imported labour for the building of the Central Pacific line. More coolies were summoned from the Orient, and by 1869, nearly 15,000 were helping to push the railroad through to Utah from the west. They worked for a pittance compared to the wages demanded by the Irish and other whites labouring on behalf of the Union Pacific railroad, which was advancing to meet them from the east.

When the great labour was completed and America was at last traversed from east to west by the railroad, the Chinese work-force that had built much of this marvel flooded into the already strained labour market of San Francisco. Once again, they faced the animosity of unskilled whites competing for work. In particular, they became the scapegoats of the Workingmen's Party, a strong-arm political group that was substantially Irish in membership. Distilling their programme in a brutal slogan, "The

A young bongo player makes an expert assessment of the day's take. Although San Francisco has absorbed at least 90,000 blacks since the Second World War, it has managed to avoid the violent racial antagonisms that have afflicted other Californian cities, such as Oakland, across the Bay, where open warfare raged between police and the para-military Black Panther movement during the 1960s.

Chinese Must Go", the Workingmen's Party in 1877 sacked the Chinese quarter of the town, producing days of riot.

But it was Congress in Washington, mindful of California's voting power, that produced the harshest measures against the Chinese of San Francisco. A series of laws enacted between 1882 and the turn of the century virtually stopped further immigration. One measure even prevented Chinese residents who were temporarily out of the country from returning to their homes in America. Not until 1943 were the repressive Exclusion Acts finally repealed.

Faced with such difficulties, the Chinese fell back on their own resources. They formed the Chinese Consolidated Benevolent Association, popularly known as the Six Companies. Made up of elected officials, the association looked after the interests of all the people from the ancestral districts of Canton: the Hing Yeung district, the Shew Hing, the Hop Wo, the King Chow, the Yeong Wo, the Sam Yup and the Yan Wo. It served several purposes at once. Its officials acted as a tribunal among the Chinese themselves. They served as intermediaries between individual Chinese and the American courts, whose workings were frequently obscure to an immigrant with little or no understanding of English. They kept a census of those who dwelled in Chinatown. They authorized and ran various welfare services of their own. And they arranged (in secret, since the practice was frowned upon by American law) for the transport of dead Chinese to their ancestral home. Virtually nothing could happen inside Chinatown without the sanction, or at least the knowledge, of the Six Companies.

The tongs were another matter, though their significance has usually been misunderstood by Westerners, who have linked them exclusively with the bloody tong wars in Chinatown in the years before the 1906 earthquake. *Tong* in Chinese simply means "association" or "meeting place"; and a church, for example, is commonly called Fook Yum Tong (a place for preaching the gospel). Tong was therefore a term that might be attached to many Chinese organizations without involvement in violence of any kind. But the word was adopted by groups of racketeers and thugs in the Chinese community who controlled every kind of unsavoury activity that would make money. The Kwong Dak Tong trafficked in girls; the Hip Shing Tong ran the gambling joints. The tongs also went in for extortion and protection rackets and succeeded in penetrating the respectable Chinese business community.

In the 1880s the tongs broke into open warfare among themselves, in a struggle to take over the leadership of Chinatown. All manner of weapons were used in their mortal fights, but the hatchet became the most notorious one. The feuding continued unabated for 20 years or more, until the 1906 earthquake literally wrecked the city and forced the Chinese, in common with other San Franciscans, to concentrate on putting life together again.

Ever since, Chinatown has been much quieter, although San Franciscans became concerned in the 1970s that a kind of tong warfare was breaking out again. There were more than 40 killings in the Chinese community between 1969 and 1978, the bloodiest act occurring on September 4, 1977, when hoodlums crashed in upon diners at the Golden Dragon Restaurant in Chinatown and shot five young people dead on the spot.

A new spate of immigration in recent years has tended to exacerbate, if not inspire, violence of various kinds by gangs. Ever since American immigration laws were liberalized in 1965, Chinese—virtually all of them from Taiwan and Hong Kong—have been entering San Francisco at the rate of about 1,500 a year. Many of the newcomers have suffered the traditional woes of all immigrants. They have started off in debt to those who paid their passages to the States; and they have found work and housing hard to come by. All these classic conditions—compounded by the frustrations of the language problem—have been an impetus for turning Chinese adolescents to gang warfare and other forms of crime.

Chinatown remains the ethnic province of those who occupy the lower rungs of the community's social and economic order. But Chinatown is also the place where Chinese trade is concentrated most heavily, where Chinese cinemas and other entertainments are to be found, and where the people themselves congregate most thickly any day of the year.

If you enter Chinatown from downtown San Francisco, you do so under a huge oriental arch that has been placed across Grant Avenue. It sets the tone for what you find within. Some visitors may think that the main thoroughfare of Chinatown is a little too contrived, but I am not one of them. To be sure, the buildings here are barely three-quarters of a century old, but they have a flair that makes time immaterial. Dragons are entwined around pillars; eaves jut tipsily as though made of bamboo; and the colour scheme consists mostly of reds and greens and gilt. The riot of chinoiserie comes off marvellously well in the cramped atmosphere of Grant Avenue—one of San Francisco's narrower streets—and is just as successful elsewhere in Chinatown, where very little has been spared this painting with an oriental brush. What looks like a pagoda turns out to be a bank. Even the telephone booths are constructed in ancient Chinese style, and the lettering in Chinese announces that here is the "Electric Voice House".

A great deal of trade here is pointedly directed at the tourists who throng the streets during any season of the year. But just as much—maybe even more—belongs to the Chinese themselves. Every morning, the top end of Grant Avenue sees the arrival of a tanker truck from which fish are scooped live and taken into a shop nearby; and there, for the next few hours, men in white aprons help each customer to pick a live fish, and then butcher it on the spot. A bit further down the road is an emporium that specializes in ivory goods and much more mysterious things; in its windows you may see glass containers holding the preserved carcasses of small deer, rodents, snakes and various other creatures, which once had a part to play in traditional Chinese medicine.

But the most fascinating trade in all Chinatown, for my money, is that conducted by herbalists in two or three narrow little shops. Behind their counters, a multitude of small drawers rise to the ceiling; back there you will generally find a couple of old men (I suspect it takes a long time to become expert in the Chinese herbal craft) carefully making up prescriptions, hour after hour. The drawers are filled with hundreds of different roots and barks and leaves ready to be mixed and later drunk, like tea; there are dozens of ginsengs alone. The herbalists have small, hand-held weighing scales, paper in which to wrap things up—and, beyond these tools, little else but their own accumulated knowledge of what has cured which ailment or relieved which soreness for thousands of years.

On Stockton Street, a notice-board outside the Presbyterian Church indicates a bridgehead between Western and Oriental ways: Sunday services—announces the board—will be held at 10.15 a.m. and 7.30 p.m. in English, at 9.30 a.m. in Mandarin, and at noon in Cantonese. English is scarcely known in the Confucian Temple just up the hill. Yet here, too—amidst the whiff of joss sticks and the votary offerings of fruit and sweetmeats, the richly carved figures and the gleaming brass gongs—there is a meeting of cultures: a closed-circuit television screen allows anyone in the temple upstairs to observe all who enter the door on Stockton Street.

Although Stockton stands to one side of the main flow of Chinatown, it is, in one sense, the centre. In a building alongside the Confucian Temple, the 55 elected directors of the Six Companies continue to meet regularly to sort out the problems of Chinatown. The Companies no longer have the power they once did; but quite apart from the numerous welfare works they direct, they still carry weight within the community, and still act as a tribunal of sorts when disputes occur among the various law-abiding groups. Just now and again, they even arrange for Chinese bodies to be disinterred from American cemeteries and transported home across the Pacific. The directors sit at long tables beneath a portrait of a benign Sun Yat-sen, the revolutionary leader who released China from the crushing power of the Manchus early in the 20th Century. Homage to the father-figure of modern China is by no means confined to this building. On October 10 each year, a great parade starts on Portsmouth Square and wends its way through the streets to mark the birth of Sun Yat-sen's Chinese Republic in 1911. But in recent years, on October 1, there has been another celebration in Chinatown, to remind everyone of the revolution led by Mao Tse-tung.

Neither of these occasions, however, remotely compares with the celebration of the Chinese New Year. According to the Chinese lunar calendar and the pronouncements of the ancient philosopher Tung Fang-so, this takes place on the first day of the new moon after the sun enters the sign of Aquarius—in other words, sometime between January 20 and February 20. Each year is symbolized by an animal, in a cycle of 12: thus the Year of the Horse is followed by the Year of the Ram and, one after the other, the Monkey, Rooster, Dog, Boar, Rat, Ox, Tiger, Hare, Dragon and Serpent. Then the cycle begins again.

On whichever day New Year falls, its coming is heralded a week or more before, when the first firecracker splits the air of Chinatown. The noise builds up to a crescendo in the days that follow. Youngsters toss crackers down from balconies or throw them down side alleys to make passers-by jump, and Portsmouth Square crackles like a musketry range. A funfair takes over the square, turning it into a giddy and rowdy place; but somehow a handful of old gentlemen still manage to concentrate on their checkers and their mah-jong at the tables fixed for this purpose under the trees. Elsewhere, Chinatown's tradesmen work at fever pitch as house-wives bustle from shop to shop to collect the food they will need for the family banquet that traditionally welcomes the New Year.

The official celebrations start with a pageant downtown in Union Square. Thereafter, the jollifications continue for another week—an indoor carnival here, a Miss Chinatown contest there, dancers in lion costumes drawing crowds wherever they appear. All these are merely warm-ups for the big parade at the end of the week, when San Francisco turns out in force to watch the Chinese go by. The parade begins after sunset and takes hours to make its way through the city in a great loop. Bands and gongs, firecrackers and flares; all enliven the procession, but what most people wait for is the famous 150-foot-long dragon with 50 pairs of human legs carrying along its articulated body. It glows with the light of lamps from within; its head is very fearsome indeed; and a posse of young men at the front guide those inside the beast as they twist this way and that, rampaging down the streets. The non-Chinese on the crowded sidewalks and reviewing stands point and gape and laugh. So do those to whom Chinatown especially belongs. But here and there you may see, on some elderly Chinese face, an expression that is different from all the rest, stirred by some distant folk memory of ancient Canton.

Leave Chinatown in the direction of the Pacific and you come to the area where most of San Francisco's 90,000 or so blacks reside. Fillmore Street, running from north to south, marks the beginning of the Western Addition, which is known to its inhabitants simply as the Fillmore. If you start walking down from the north end, you pass through colonies of people who may have come from Norway or Korea or any other land; but, from Bush Street to Geary Street and spreading to the west, the people are mostly black. Some of the property is crumbling, and much of it is the oldest in San Francisco, for this part of the Fillmore was spared the ravages of the 1906 holocaust.

Sinuous dragons writhe up pagoda-shaped street lamps (above) on Grant Avenue in Chinatown, providing a picturesque link with the past for San Francisco's largest minority group. For many Chinese in the city, even today's news comes in familiar form: San Francisco has two locally published Chinese-language dailies, the "Chinese Times" (right) and "Young China", which reach a total of 18,000 readers every day.

There were blacks in San Francisco from the earliest days, and they campaigned alongside the Irish and a lot of other whites against the immigration of Chinese to provide cheap labour for the railroad. More blacks came up from Texas after the First World War, but at the beginning of the Second World War, San Francisco still had only 4,000— which meant that its black population was proportionately smaller than that of any other city in the United States. However, that figure soared after 1942 as blacks arrived to work in armaments factories around the Bay. They found, in contrast to what was then accepted practice in the South, that their children were not segregated from white kids in schools.

The conflict between blacks and whites was scarcely a local issue at all until the years following the Second World War. And when social protest throughout America was at its height in the 1960s, the frictions came to a head across the Bay in Oakland much more than in San Francisco itself. It was there that Huey Newton and Bobby Seale founded the Black Panther Party for Self-Defense in 1966, which young Eldridge Cleaver joined within a few months after his release from prison, where he had been serving a sentence for assault, and writing his apologia *Soul on Ice*.

The Panthers quickly became famous in the black ghetto of Oakland for their shadowing of the local police patrols. Whenever the police arrested a black man on the streets, Panthers would suddenly materialize—perhaps with a gun in one hand, a law book in the other—inform the arrested man of his legal rights, and disappear again. Before long, open warfare had been declared between the Panthers and the police; and when Newton was convicted of shooting a police officer in 1967, he became a national symbol, a hero of America's blacks and radical whites alike.

The year 1968 was the most dramatic of all in a tortured decade for the United States. In April, Martin Luther King was assassinated down in Tennessee. Within a week, the Panther's treasurer, Bobby Hutton, was killed in a shoot-out with the Oakland police, and Cleaver was captured in the same affray. Released on a writ of habeas corpus, Cleaver began to campaign as a presidential candidate, rousing the predominantly white students of Berkeley to paroxysms of defiance against the established order and eventually causing J. Edgar Hoover, chief of the Federal Bureau of Investigation, to characterize the Panthers as "the greatest threat to the internal security of this country". The Panthers had certainly become a focal point of rebellion, and their newspaper achieved a circulation of 150,000 copies a week. And yet, from that moment the fortunes of the Panthers began to wane. Before the end of the year, Cleaver was involved in another police confrontation and fled to Canada, later travelling to Cuba before finding a haven of sorts in Algiers. By the time he returned to San Francisco Bay almost a decade later, the old Panther leadership had split into mutually hostile factions.

The party itself had, however, achieved a sort of respectability. One of its most prominent members, Elaine Brown, was a delegate to the 1976 Democratic Convention. The Panthers had helped to elect Oakland's first black mayor in 1977. They were running a number of welfare services well thought of by blacks and whites alike. Their Oakland Community School was attended by 150 children between the ages of two-and-a-half and 12 years old, and the educational results were far more impressive than those obtained in other schools of the city. This is not to say that the roots of racial conflict in the Bay area disappeared. The black man still feels himself under-privileged compared with the white and as long as this resentment is there, confrontation remains a possibility.

But if amity is to prevail, then a great deal will be due to the lasting influence of the Glide Memorial Church, which is located in the heart of San Francisco, but whose amiable tentacles have spread around the city and, indeed, around the Bay. Glide may well be unique (it is certainly rare) on several counts. It has become, above everything else, a genuinely multi-racial and multi-social experiment, originated and developed by a charismatic black minister, the Reverend Cecil Williams.

The building on Ellis Street is labelled a Methodist church. But I doubt whether the Methodists or any other Christian denomination in the world have anything to compare with this place of worship. Until 1963 it was no different from any other church, its small congregation dutifully abiding by the orthodoxies of their faith. Then Cecil Williams arrived from Texas by way of Kansas City, and things began to change fast. He was invited to the Glide Memorial Church by its board of directors to become Minister of Involvement (which indicates the frame of mind they were already in). From the outset he involved himself in the crusade for civil rights. He took a planeload of San Franciscans to Selma, Alabama, to march in a demonstration with Martin Luther King. He formed an outfit called Citizens Alert, which was designed to support blacks, homosexuals and prostitutes in their brushes with the police.

Within three years, Cecil Williams had so impressed his bishop that he was made Minister of Glide—and the old place was never to be the same again. Altar, cross and choir loft were soon flung out of the building and this turbulent man of the cloth was preaching from the back of the church, where those who didn't like what he had to say would have to look him in the eye as they hurried out to the relatively undisturbing atmosphere of the streets. Many of Glide's stalwarts left its congregation for good; but before long their empty seats were filled by others, and people were standing in its aisles.

The keynote of Glide was soon expressed in a poster hanging on a wall in the offices below the church itself, where a multi-racial staff began co-ordinating the great array of social welfare programmes administered by the church. "Celebration," the poster proclaimed, "is when you come to the conclusion that LIFE after birth and before death is more important

than life after death. Right on!" The word "celebration" at Glide signified what other Christians called church services, but the proceedings there on Sunday mornings bore no resemblance to anything else I have ever seen in church. I found that you had to arrive well before the appointed hour to get a seat. On a platform at the front of the church, a jazz band was belting out soul music. Behind them, a psychedelic cascade of portraits and symbols cast by a light projector swivelled frantically across the wall.

The people streaming into the hall seemed to represent every race of mankind as well as every segment of San Francisco's motley society. Elderly ladies with blue-rinsed hair and white-gloved hands (churchgoers incarnate in their Sunday best) took their places alongside Hippie-looking couples in leather jackets and blue jeans. The first cry of "Hallelujah!" arose from one of the pews at the front and I traced it to an old black fellow with a beatific smile upon his face. Alongside him a white man sat, dreamily absorbing the music, his head propped on his arm. He looked like a bank manager, in spite of his open-necked shirt. A pair of nuns took their places in the pew across the aisle.

More figures appeared on the platform—members of Glide's full-time staff. Two of the most senior were Japanese-Americans, who spent their childhood in those wartime internment camps. A choir assembled in a haphazard sort of way, and soon we heard them backing a black girl whose voice and verve reminded one of the great gospel singer Mahalia Jackson. By the time Williams appeared on stage (there was no other word for it by now), the whole place was rocking with excitement.

The Reverend came on from the wings, clapping as he strode in—a tall, bearded figure in rhinestoned boots and an African *dashiki*; he had long since abandoned the collar of his trade. From that moment on, all eyes were upon him, whether he sat below the band listening to them and the singers perform, whether he was exhorting all the visitors to the church to stand up and be acclaimed as friends, or whether he was striding up and down the aisles preaching his message. Essentially, that message was one of hope. He told the congregation to be proud of themselves, for each of them was as good as anyone around. He told them to get close together, never to be hung-up. He told them many things that would come as manna to a hard-pressed soul, and he did it in a way that was easy to idolize for he had the presence of a great actor.

Williams was not always fair to orthodox Christianity, but his congregation knew well enough that the established churches deserved most of his gibes. "The Christian church has been talking for years about love," he said, delivering the last word in a long and mocking drawl. "Well I'm tired of people saying we got to luuuuuuuuv!" and he shook his head of Afro hair, patronizing the establishment, until his audience rocked with laughter down in the aisles. Then he offered them a battle cry: "Don't tell me! Show me!" The applause was deafening.

When the Sunday celebration came to an end, nobody moved until the Reverend and two acolytes had bounded to the entrance first. It took some time for the congregation to get out to the street because at the door —instead of receiving a deodorized Christian smile and a ritual shaking of the hand—each person got from Cecil Williams a whole-hearted hug full of warmth. These people of all races took that warmth out into the different parts of San Francisco; and the city could not avoid being influenced by it. It seemed to me that if the Mission Dolores was a deeply moving place because of its careful fidelity to the oldest of Christian ways, the Glide Memorial Church was inspiring because it held out genuine hope of beatitudes yet unattained.

7

Serene and Indifferent to Fate

There is a paradox in the life of San Francisco. Rarely has a city shown such confidence in the future, but with so little cause. If San Francisco's nerve-ends constantly tingle at the prospect of another major earthquake —and scientists predict one is inevitable—this concern is rarely expressed. Yet people not only live on the edge of catastrophe, they also have a perfect illustration of what may happen when disaster strikes.

Whenever a San Franciscan pauses to consider his city's history, one date dominates all others: Wednesday, April 18, 1906. On that day the city was wrecked by one of the most devastating earthquakes of all time and then engulfed by fire. The Richter Magnitude Scale, by which the severity of earth tremors is measured, was not devised until 1935, but seismographic records have enabled scientists to apply the scale to earthquakes that took place as far back as 1904. The magnitudes since then have generally ranged from 3 to 8, and the worst earthquakes ever recorded have reached only 8.8 or 8.9. What San Francisco suffered in 1906 was the equivalent of a Richter reading of 8.3.

The city's ordeal began at 5.13 a.m., when a pale crescent moon still hung in the dawn sky. Horses had been restless for hours, snorting and fretting in stables throughout the city, but the people were sleeping peacefully. One of them was the Italian tenor, Enrico Caruso, who had sung Don José in *Carmen* at the Opera House before going to bed in the Palace Hotel on Market Street. The earthquake started 200 miles to the north. Travelling at two miles a second (more than 7,000 mph), it smashed through stretches of the California coastline and ripped along the sea-bed beneath the Pacific. Seconds before it struck the city, its kick-back effect caused a schooner 150 miles offshore to leap in the water, mystifying her captain and crew, who could find no reason for the shock. Seismographs began to quiver as far away as Moscow. A policeman patrolling San Francisco's produce district heard a deep rumble and then saw the earthquake coming up Washington Street. "The whole street was undulating," he said later. "It was as if the waves of the ocean were coming towards me, billowing as they came."

The bell in the tower of old St. Mary's Church in Chinatown began to toll crazily, and its sound was echoed by other bells across the city as the tremor mounted in intensity. It died down after 40 seconds and then, after a 10-second respite, resumed with even greater violence for a further 25 seconds. A journalist, awakened by the first shock, heard a roar of bricks and girders falling and through his window saw the 12-storey St.

As the city burns after the calamitous earthquake on April 18, 1906, firemen operate a puny fire engine in downtown California Street, using some of the scanty water supplies left after the rupture of the city's mains. Fires raged out of control for three days as desperate fire-fighters pumped water from cisterns and sewers—and even beat at the wind-fanned flames with their hoses and tunic jackets.

Outside crazily tilted homes on the day after the 1906 earthquake, two carts wait to evacuate residents and their goods to camps in the city's parks and squares.

Francis Hotel swaying like a tree in a high wind. The rear of his own building collapsed on to a row of wooden houses, its masonry crashing through their roofs as though they were made of tissue paper.

In the Palace Hotel, Caruso's conductor, Alfred Hertz, found the tenor weeping hysterically in bed, terrified that the shock of what he had just endured would ruin his voice. Hertz opened the window of Caruso's suite and told the singer to stand by it and test his vocal chords. Caruso chose a passage from Umberto Giordano's *Fedora*, the opera in which he had swept to fame eight years before. People who had rushed out to the street in panic looked up and applauded wildly. The great man appeared to be showing that he, at least, was not afraid.

By the time the last tremor had subsided, much of the city was smashed, including the water mains—which proved to be the worst blow of all: worse by far than the destruction of City Hall and the Opera House; worse even than the death of the city's fire chief, who was fatally injured after plunging through three collapsing floors of his own fire station on Bush Street. Within 17 minutes of the quake, some 50 fires broke out downtown from overturned stoves and fractured gas pipes. This was the real disaster of San Francisco in 1906. Of all the damage to the city, only 20 per cent was directly attributable to the quake; the rest was due to the fire.

San Franciscans who had left their homes in alarm when the earth shook beneath their beds now began to retreat across the city as columns of black smoke thickened into clouds that would darken that day; and the next; and the one after that. Jack London, who immediately rushed down to the stricken city from his home in Sonoma County to report the disaster for a magazine, found that Union Square had been turned into a makeshift refugee camp. But the encroaching fire soon caused the refugees to move on again.

Lacking water, the city's fire-fighters decided the blaze could only be brought under control by dynamiting houses to create firebreaks. But the dynamite was in the hands of inexperienced soldiers and at first they started more fires than they stopped. They had been called out by the acting commander of the garrison in the Presidio, Brigadier General Frederick Funston, who impetuously declared martial law on his own initiative, a step that could properly be taken by the President of the United States alone. The ineptitude of the apprentice dynamiters was not, however, to be the worst failing of Funston's soldiery that week. Armed to prevent looting, they were over-zealous; and before long there were stories of troops shooting people on the spot—sometimes those who were merely trying to salvage their own goods.

San Francisco that week was a beleaguered city, bearing the marks more customary in one ravaged by war. The telephone system went out of action on the first morning; the city's only contact with the outside world was maintained by a single telegraph operator in Union Square, who kept tapping out messages by Morse Code until just after 2 a.m., when fire forced him to abandon the building. It took 19 hours for the first relief train carrying food and medical supplies to arrive from Los Angeles.

By then, the fire was completely out of hand, spreading north from the poor quarter below Market Street and west towards the broad ribbon of Van Ness Avenue, where houses were eventually shelled by artillery in order to prevent the flames from fanning further. In the great wedge of San Francisco between those two thoroughfares—five square miles or so —practically everything was incinerated. The flames advanced almost as far as the Bay, whose water could be pumped through hoses to save the buildings nearby. A few buildings on the highest ground survived, but the great mansions of the railroad barons on Nob Hill were not spared. Mark Hopkins' place was the first to burn; Collis Huntington's, solidly constructed of stone, took longest to be devoured by the flames, though neither man witnessed the event (all the Big Four had died by 1901). Chinatown was wiped out and so was the business centre of the city.

While A. P. Giannini was saving the wealth of his little Bank of Italy with the aid of a horse and cart, the employees of the much larger Crocker Bank were conveying a million dollars' worth of bonds along Market Street in a wheelbarrow, placing them in a boat hired by the directors, and sailing this vessel to the middle of the Bay, where it dropped anchor until the fire was over. A priest, Father Charles Ramm, was scaling the spire of St. Mary's Cathedral to beat out flames and save the building. The actor John Barrymore got drunk and remained thus until the last flame was doused. The fire raged so long that many of the refugee citizens, encamped in Golden Gate Park and elsewhere out of its range, began to pose for pictures with their smoking city as a backdrop. It was not until Friday, when a change of wind started fanning the fire across ground it had already covered, that the turning point came. When Saturday dawned and the horror ended, the heart of San Francisco was smouldering rubble. Then, for the first time since the beginning of the earthquake and the fire, it started to rain.

The cost of the disaster was high. More than half the population— 250,000—were left without homes, and 28,000 buildings were destroyed. From the rubble 315 bodies were recovered. A further 352 were never found and relatives had no means of knowing whether those missing had been crushed in the earthquake, burned by the flames, or shot by trigger-happy soldiers. The financial loss was estimated at around $500 million, of which 20 per cent was never recovered. Only half a dozen of the 65 major insurance companies involved—four American and two English—met the claims of their clients in full and without delay; the rest spent months or even years trying to avoid their liabilities, though most of the money claimed was paid eventually.

Zig-zagging up the northern slopes of San Bruno mountain half a mile south of San Francisco, these houses were built in the early 1960s during the rapid expansion of Daly City. This exurb sprang up along the 700-mile-long San Andreas Fault, source of dozens of earth tremors every year. Although hit in 1957 by the most severe shock in the San Francisco area since 1906, the population of Daly City increased by almost 50 per cent in the following decade.

The calm waters of Richardson Bay, five miles north of San Francisco, provide safe anchorage for a wealthy houseboat community. The inhabitants, like their neighbours in nearby Sausalito, enjoy superb views of the Marin County hills bordering the Bay and also have quick access to the city via Highway 101, whose elevated lanes sweep past in the background.

In the months after the earthquake, San Francisco began the task of clearing up, housing its homeless meanwhile in tents supplied by the military and in temporary wooden shacks. Most of the debris was carried away by trains, running on tracks laid over the streets, and pushed into the Bay. It was almost a year before all the rubble was removed, but in that time the city received massive aid from all over the United States and from many other parts of the world. It came in the form of food, medicine, blankets and other supplies, as well as cash totalling $9 million.

Stimulated by this money and payments from the insurance companies, a massive building boom began. The number of construction workers employed in the city more than tripled and the earnings of skilled artisans rose to heights not touched since Gold-Rush days. Within three years 20,500 new buildings had been put up, most of them superior in design, workmanship and materials to those they replaced. By 1909 more than half the steel-frame structures in the United States stood in San Francisco and the city's real estate value was assessed at 50 per cent more than before the earthquake. In this incredibly short time San Francisco had become a thriving metropolis once more.

Much of the rebuilding might have been avoided if this had been a less optimistic place. No one could claim that what happened in 1906 came out of the blue. From the earliest days, sections of the city had burned down so often that fire-fighting was part of its spirit. Precautions, alas, were not so close to its soul. Only a few months before, the National Board of Fire Underwriters had criticized the city's water supply as inadequate for a major conflagration, but their recommendations went mostly unheeded.

Furthermore, of all places on earth, San Francisco might have been expected to take all possible steps to protect itself against the effects of

Across the Bay from San Francisco, a rainbow soars into the heavens as the evening sun spangles windows on Treasure Island and the Berkeley campus beyond.

earthquakes. In the preceding half century, well over 400 tremors of varying intensity had occurred in and around the growing city on the Bay. Twice—in 1865 and 1868—the quakes had been severe enough to cause both damage and fire. Earthquakes happen to be a fact of everyday life in California, which lies on the great seismic belt that circles the Pacific Ocean and is responsible for 80 per cent of all earth tremors. The state is fissured with hundreds of fault lines. The majority are of little consequence —as, indeed, are most of the tremors themselves. But two of the major fault lines run parallel to one another on either side of San Francisco, slanting from north-west to south-east.

The Hayward Fault, the lesser of the two, strikes through Berkeley and Oakland on the far side of the Bay. The San Andreas Fault extends from Cape Mendocino in northern California and follows the coast southward, now on land and now under the sea. It passes outside the Golden Gate and comes ashore just south of the San Francisco city boundary, where it cuts through Daly City before continuing down to the Gulf of California —a distance of 700 miles in all. The San Andreas Fault—less than a hundred yards wide at some places and up to a mile across at others—is the dividing line between two geophysical plates: huge, rigid masses of the earth's crust that float on the hot, viscous magma many miles below ground level. One of these plates is believed to underlie the whole North Pacific and a slice of the California coast; the other underlies the rest of North America and the Western Atlantic. The Pacific plate is shifting north-west and the North American plate in the opposite direction, the one moving on average about two inches a year in relation to the other. When they grind together along the San Andreas Fault, California has earthquakes.

Although this is a continual process, only one in 10,000 tremors does any great damage to the Golden State. But in 1906 the plates had been jammed together for a long time. Tremendous pressure built up and suddenly catapulted each plate into a massive displacement. In just over a minute, the ground beneath San Francisco shifted a distance of 20 feet. On a minor scale, the same movements are also continually occurring along the Hayward Fault and along the much smaller fractures. But above all others, the San Andreas is the one to worry about.

Earthquake-watching is carried out more assiduously and more expertly around San Francisco Bay than almost anywhere else in the world. The United States Geological Survey's National Center for Earthquake Research was established at Menlo Park in 1966; and at Berkeley the University of California has a seismographic station that keeps track of quakes on every continent. Information is regularly exchanged with the experts of other countries in an attempt to work out patterns of earthquake activity. So careful is this international watch that at night, when the staff at the Berkeley seismographic station are not on duty, a buzzer sounds in the campus police headquarters if the instruments record a shock; and some weary scientist is hauled out of bed to calculate where the epicentre lies and to notify federal or state agencies of possible dangers. For example, if the epicentre is beneath the Pacific, there may be a tidal wave and experts can predict when and where it may strike.

As a result of such constant monitoring, a great deal has been discovered about earthquakes. The scientists at Berkeley now know that California is especially prone to them in the autumn. They can predict where an earthquake is likely to be and what magnitude it is likely to reach. But they are scrupulously insistent on the limits of their skill and cannot confidently say exactly when it will happen. According to the director of the Berkeley station, the next big one in California "could be tonight or tomorrow—it will certainly be within the next 50 years".

In spite of the perpetual danger, California has been astonishingly slow to take even the most basic precautions. After 1906 a number of building codes were drafted to ensure the use of earthquake-resistant construction methods—notably the Field Act of 1933 and the Garrison Act of 1939— but they were not rigorously enforced until more than 30 years later and virtually none of the codes applied to buildings put up before the statutes became law. When the San Fernando Valley was badly shaken in 1971 by a quake of 6.6 magnitude, hospital buildings at Sylmar, near Los Angeles, collapsed, killing 45 people. The buildings had been put up in 1926 and had never been strengthened. Residential areas were heavily damaged, too, and freeway bridges fell down.

Since then some more serious attempts have been made to face up to the danger. The California state government has spent several million dollars running steel hawsers beneath vulnerable sections of freeway so that, in the event of another major shock, the roads would merely sag instead of collapsing. Schools of sub-standard construction have been closed. Anyone wishing to build within a mile of a fault line is now obliged to get a scientific opinion about the suitability of the geological foundation. Sand, artificial fill and alluvium are known to be less stable than solid rock, and if the developer receives an unfavourable report, he is not allowed to proceed. But the handicap facing the authorities is that, in the final analysis, it is the people themselves who decide how safe their buildings are to be. It would cost a very large sum of money to protect every structure adequately from the effects of earthquake, and the money can only be raised with the sanction of the taxpayers. Too often, say the experts, the citizens just don't want to know.

Given these attitudes, the most that the experts can do is to make contingency plans for the day they hope will never come in their lifetimes. San Francisco has a small team constantly refining an emergency operations plan that is designed to deal with any kind of disaster—from nuclear attack to inundation of the city by Pacific tidal waves. This document is

dense with the procedures to be adopted in this or that circumstance, with charts showing the various chains of command, and with general observations about the behaviour of human beings in times of great stress and peril. It seems that we do not, as a rule, rush about in a mad panic if we are told precisely how dreadful things are. On the contrary, morale in a disaster-stricken community tends to be high and the task of the authorities is to harness it to useful activity.

Believing that a community's chances of survival are higher if it is well-informed, the disaster planners have projected some effects on San Francisco today if it should be struck by another earthquake with a magnitude as great as the one of 1906. Casualties would be lightest if the earthquake struck when the 4.6 million people in the nine counties of the Bay area were at home in bed. They would be heaviest at about 4.30 in the afternoon, when the rush hour starts in San Francisco and many people are out in the open or travelling underground by BART. At that time there could be as many as 10,000 dead and 40,000 injured badly enough to need hospital treatment. Even if no hospitals were damaged (a doubtful proposition, since 44 per cent of hospitals in the Bay area were built at least partially before 1933), such a large number of casualties would stretch the city's resources almost to the limit.

If the earthquake were along the San Andreas Fault, more than 10,000 family houses would be made uninhabitable and more than 36,000 people might be homeless. If it ran along the Hayward Fault, the number of damaged houses would be the same, but the homeless could be as

A section of a 200-foot-long outdoor mural in the Western Addition district represents longshoremen marching past the Ferry Building during a Depression-era strike while a top-hatted industrialist, getting a shoeshine, ignores the pleas of a hungry child. The mural, illustrating the full sweep of San Francisco's social history, was painted by neighbourhood artists commissioned by the city.

many as 57,000, owing to the greater number of apartment buildings in that danger zone; the BART subway running beneath the waters of the Bay would be closed indefinitely. A San Andreas shock would put one in every four freeways in Marin, San Francisco, San Mateo and Santa Clara Counties out of action, together with the Golden Gate, Bay and San Mateo Bridges. San Francisco's airport would be unusable for weeks.

All radio and television in the city and in San Mateo County would be blacked out for 24 hours before transmitters could be repaired. Up to 50 per cent of the telephones in the Bay area would be out of order for an indefinite period. A quarter of the city's fire stations would be damaged, though nearly 90 per cent of all equipment and manpower would be on the streets within 15 minutes of the shock. This does not mean, however, that the fire-fighters would achieve 90 per cent effectiveness, "since some problems—such as blocked streets, ruptured water distribution lines and poor communications—would adversely affect operations".

Long before the 1906 earthquake, Bret Harte thought of San Francisco as a city "serene and indifferent to fate". The description seems to become more appropriate with the passage of time. San Francisco sails contentedly on in the sunlight of its dreams, Serenissima of the West. I am sure this spirit is due partly to the city's amazing confidence in its capacity for survival. But there is another force at work. San Francisco is set amid one of the most beautiful landscapes on earth. You need only raise your eyes northwards, past the Golden Gate, to see the splendid hills of Marin County. Travelling around San Francisco Bay, you do not have to go far to discover the charms of inlet and cove, headland and wooded slope. The shores of this inland sea are dotted with small communities like Port Costa and Sausalito, which are as picturesque in their own Californian way as anything you might find on the Mediterranean. At Port Costa there is a street of clapboard houses that meanders through elm trees to the narrow passage of the Carquinez Strait. Walk along that street, which is as hobbledehoy as they come, and you may find an oil tanker cruising gently up the strait, passing between fields where cattle are raised, on its way from the Golden Gate to the refinery at Martinez.

You can drive from the very heart of San Francisco across the Golden Gate and, within the hour, find yourself in Muir Woods, below the southwestern flank of Mount Tamalpais. Here are more than 400 acres of redwood trees, by no means the most impressive collection in California but some of them growing 250 feet high along a ravine that also flourishes with laurel and oak, azalea, huckleberry and fir. And this is merely the threshold of virgin country beyond.

It is a setting that beckons all who long for utopia. So it is no surprise to discover that Sausalito is the headquarters of the *Whole Earth Catalog* people, whose publications contain a worthy mixture of politics, ecology, gadgetry, arty camerawork and strip cartoons. There is no place in the world where utopian ideals have taken root more abundantly than in San Francisco and its hinterland. This part of California is littered with experiments in living; and any new social theorist can be sure that, however outlandish his notions may seem to the majority of people, there will be some folk around ready and willing to try them out in practice.

The following list of local cults does not pretend to be exhaustive and all of them have adherents throughout the United States and in other countries as well. But I doubt very much if, in one small area of the globe, you would find such intense dedication, at one and the same time, to: Actualism, Analytical Tracking, est, Feldenkrais Functional Integration, Fischer-Hoffman Process, Gurdjieff, Human Life Styling, Integral Massage, Manipulation, Neo-Reichian Bodywork, Orgonomy, Polarity Balancing, Postural Integration, Primal Therapy, Scientology, Silva Mind Control, Synanon, Tai Chi, Theta, Yoga and Zen.

The American journalist John Gunther wrote in the 1940s that "California is stuck with so many crackpots because they can't go any further". A Californian friend of mine observed, more kindly and with a finer sense of irony, that "New Yorkers go to a psychiatrist to cope with their problems; people come here to enlarge their self-understanding."

Many of them embark on this experiment in the sympathetic atmosphere of communes, which have developed apace in recent years. How the communes see their purpose in life can be as varied as the list of cults I have given. One announces itself in a directory of communes thus: "We are now eight women and eight men living in three households, with plans for urban/rural expansion. We practise Gestalt-O-Rama, an egalitarian process of group dynamics, enhanced communication, awareness development. Also we've evolved a new family structure called Spiritual Polyfidelity, an advanced form of emotionally committed group marriage."

Another commune, advertising itself in the same directory, has this to say: "We raise our children communally, share many possessions, contribute to a communal budget, eat an organic modified vegetarian diet, work together in our non-hierarchical business and co-operate on housework and maintenance of our communal vehicle. Some of us are bi-sexual, others are heterosexual. We strive for open relationships and feel uncomfortable with traditionally coupled people."

No doubt many of these people are content, though they do not strike me as being very humorous. Anyone who can solemnly declare that he has "evolved a new family structure called Spiritual Polyfidelity" is either taking himself too seriously or has been over-exposed to the propaganda of the plastics industry—which is exactly what the latter-day communards say they are trying to get away from. This earnestness and the awful jargon that goes with it is not, unfortunately, confined to the communes. It is to be found in patches throughout the Bay area. Worse, it has spread

Few individuals have done more to enhance the local landscape than the Italian-born sculptor Beniamino Bufano, whose works are displayed in many of San Francisco's open spaces. A resident of the city from 1914 until his death in 1970, Bufano often declared that the only critics he cared about were children, and so he designed his tantalizingly undefined animal figures to stimulate their imagination.

Bufano steed with rider

Cat with a granite grin

Feline enigma

Penguin and offspring

Well-rounded elephant

steadily eastwards from Pacific utopia and is seeping into every corner of the English-speaking world. I only hope the jargon is untranslatable, so that non-English speakers may be spared what a Boston journalist named R. D. Rosen has identified as "psychobabble".

If there is a geographical centre of psychobabble, it is not San Francisco itself but Marin County, which starts at the northern end of the Golden Gate Bridge and includes Sausalito. Conversations hereabouts have long been thick with ambiguous words like "cool" and "into"; people speak long-windedly of "an ongoing situation" or "a value judgment"; and they borrow obscure expressions from the vocabularies of science, like "parameter" and "interface", to impress others with a knowledge they do not genuinely have. They do not understand that the purpose of language is to communicate feelings and ideas as clearly as possible and that clarity is more likely to follow when simple words are used economically, with unmistakable meaning. I imagine there is a connection between the incoherence of psychobabble and the fact that Marin has a higher divorce rate than any other county in the United States.

It will be apparent that I am irritated by this mode of speech and the cast of mind it reveals. Yet, even a fogbank of misused and superfluous words and half-baked ideas cannot hide the inventiveness and originality of the Californian search for a more fulfilling way of life. This dynamism is expressed in all kinds of ways. When I have asked San Franciscans of all sorts to talk to me about their city, they have most frequently commented that it is a nice place to live and that this is where the future lies. I have never had any doubt about the first of these two propositions. The second has puzzled me sometimes, because those who assert it most vigorously, when pressed for an explanation, have been vague about its meaning. But it seems to include the freedom to experiment with life, unfettered by the rules of orthodoxy. And that is a powerful force for optimism.

One of its most attractive manifestations is the ambitious project of urban renewal that has been transforming the downtown area of San Francisco between Jackson and Sacramento Streets. Here, where the old produce district used to be located, the Golden Gateway development and the Embarcadero Center have arisen side by side since the early Sixties, providing proof that inner cities can actually be places worth living in. There are those who lament the passing of old landmarks, but I do not think they can quibble with what they have gained in exchange.

So successful have the planners been that one could happily live in these few blocks without ever needing to leave except for a holiday. The complex includes houses, gardens, offices, restaurants, shopping precincts, recreation areas—even a hotel; and although most of the inhabitants live in apartment blocks that rise as high as 25 storeys there is none of the oppressive monotony that characterizes inner-city development elsewhere in America. There are sculptures that sometimes thrust their way through

High above an elaborate sculpture in the lobby of the Hyatt Regency Hotel, three illuminated elevator capsules hang from the 22nd floor like paper lanterns.

A phoenix, emblem of San Francisco, rises from the flames on the shoulder patch of a policeman filling out a parking ticket. The mythical bird, said to be reborn from its own funeral pyre, was chosen in 1852 to represent the city after a series of disastrous fires. The motto on the badge reads, in Spanish, "Gold in peace, Iron in war."

several levels of the shopping centres and fountains that play in otherwise arid corners of this complex.

Nowhere, however, has the architectural imagination been more strikingly applied than, in the Hyatt Regency Hotel. The Hyatt Regency contains something that should conventionally be called the hotel lobby. But "lobby" suggests a degree of confinement and that is the last sensation you feel here. Instead, the architect has produced an almost magical combination of space and activity. Beneath a skylight, he has included all the conventional features of a hotel lobby—and many things besides. A stream runs over rocks, and birds perch on the trees that are ranged along each bank. A sculptured sphere—a huge ball of filigree 40 feet high—stands in the centre of the lobby. Around the lobby and rising high above the central sculpture are tiers of balconies that lead to the 800 guest rooms. One tier leans daringly outwards, so that the facing balconies at the top are a great deal closer to one another than those at the bottom.

From each of the balconies plants descend from baskets in long skeins of green. The Hanging Gardens of Babylon must have looked something like this, though they never had anything to resemble the hotel's elevators. Delicate, lozenge-shaped vehicles of darkened glass with light glowing from within, they move up and down on the outside of the elevator shafts, in full view of the onlookers in the lobby. So silently do they move, so smoothly do they glide from floor to floor, so marvellously do they appeal to the child in us all, that the lobby watchers tend to lose all track of time. No less than 2,000 sightseers, it is estimated, come here every day, so it may fairly be said that this architectural novelty has already been raised to the status of a landmark. In the opinion of an article in the *American Institute of Architects' Journal*, "San Francisco would not be the same without it".

Perhaps the most remarkable thing about the new downtown development is that it should have been built at all. It stands on a stretch of land reclaimed from the Bay, and this was one of the areas most seriously damaged during the 1906 earthquake. The whole lot could come crashing down tomorrow. But the investment of money and imagination symbolizes San Francisco's view of life. This is a city that refuses to look on the gloomy side, no matter how disastrous the past or how uncertain the future. Now and then in San Francisco, people's awareness of the well-documented hazards becomes obvious enough. If an aircraft plunges through the sound barrier above San Francisco Bay, the sonic boom is immediately followed by a mass of telephone calls to the geophysicists at Berkeley and Menlo Park from citizens anxious to know whether the noise means The Bad News. But most of the time, although insurance companies may take a more sober view (of all San Francisco property insured against fire, only five per cent is covered against earthquake too), people in the city live as though the San Andreas Fault were something that others must answer for.

In New York it used to be possible to obtain a time check by dialling the letters NERVOUS. In San Francisco you dialled POPCORN. A small thing, but it says much about the different spirits pervading the two cities at opposite ends of America. It is San Francisco's capacity for facing life with a light heart that compels so many people to try their luck here. The young have always fallen for it and, like Sal Paradise when he was on the road, they keep on coming. If you go down to the Greyhound Bus Terminal off Market Street, you may see them arriving in ones and twos, twice each day, aboard a bus that has lumbered across the continent from New York by way of Chicago, Salt Lake City, Reno and points in between. As they climb down with their bags, they are weary and stiff. But there is a hopeful glint in their eyes and they look around them with the innocent expectancy of pilgrims who have entered the Promised Land.

An Intimacy with Wind and Water

Apparently heading out into the limitless blue of the Pacific, a hang-glider swoops over the shore near Fort Funston on the south-western fringes of the city.

From their precincts on the magnificent western shores of the United States, the people of San Francisco seem forever on the verge of taking off into the boundless freedom of ocean and sky. Something in the alluring Pacific air makes them champ at the restraints of earthbound existence, testing their skill, strength or courage in a whole range of outdoor activities. High above the restless shore, intrepid hang-gliders balance on the breeze, while the less adventurous manipulate their elaborate kites from ground level. Out in the sparkling ocean, surf-boarders slide down the shifting slopes of enormous breakers, while wind-surfers skim over the broad expanses of San Francisco Bay. Others are content simply to stretch their legs along one of the wide open beaches. As the American author William Saroyan once said: "If you're alive, you can't be bored in San Francisco."

Dwarfed by a cresting wave and overshadowed by the central span of the Golden Gate Bridge, surf-boarders brave strong currents at the mouth of the Bay.

Calmer waters inside the Bay provide perfect conditions for wind-surfers. The sport, enjoyed throughout the U.S. and Europe, originated in California in 1966.

Eight reproductions of the Stars and Stripes make for a patriotic box kite.

Two youngsters fly their kites at Twin Peaks. The observation point, south of the downtown area, offers a grand panorama of the city looking towards the Bay.

Matching their own high spirits to the surging rollers, a young couple break into an impromptu sprint along the spray-swept Pacific shore near Seal Rocks.

Bibliography

Bancroft, Hubert Howe, *History of the Pacific States of America,* vols. 13, 14 and 15. A. L. Bancroft & Company, San Francisco, 1884, 1885.

Bean, Walton, *Boss Ruef's San Francisco.* University of California Press, Berkeley, 1952.

Braasch, Barbara J., ed., *Sunset Travel Guide to Northern California.* Lane Publishing Co., Menlo Park, California, 1970.

Bronson, William, *The Earth Shook, The Sky Burned.* Doubleday & Company, New York, 1959.

Charters, Ann, *Kerouac.* André Deutsch Ltd., London, 1974.

Cowan, Robert Ernest, *Forgotten Characters of Old San Francisco.* Los Angeles, Ward Ritchie Press, California, 1938.

Davie, Michael, *In the Future Now.* Hamish Hamilton Ltd., London, 1972.

Dickson, Samuel, *The Streets of San Francisco.* Stanford University Press, California, 1955.

Dillon, Richard H., *Embarcadero.* Coward-McCann, New York, 1959.

Dillon, Richard H., *The Hatchet Men: The Story of the Tong Wars in San Francisco.* Coward-McCann, New York, 1962.

Doss, Margaret Patterson, *San Francisco at your Feet.* Grove Press, Inc., New York, 1974.

Frommer, Arthur, *Guide to San Francisco, 1977-78.* The Frommer/Pasmantier Publishing Corporation, New York, 1977.

Genthe, Arnold, *Pictures of Old Chinatown.* Moffatt Yard and Company, New York, 1909.

Gentry, Curt, *The Dolphin Guide to San Francisco and the Bay Area.* Doubleday & Company, Inc., New York, 1969.

Gilliam, Harold, *San Francisco Bay.* Doubleday & Company, Inc., New York, 1957.

Ginsberg, Allen, *Howl and Other Poems.* City Lights Press, San Francisco, 1976.

Girdner, Audrie, and Loftis, Anne, *The Great Betrayal: The evacuation of the Japanese-Americans during World War II.* The Macmillan Company, London, 1969.

Gold Star Graphics, *Inside Alcatraz.* San Bruno, California, 1974.

Hansen, Gladys, ed., *San Francisco: A Guide to the Bay and Its Cities.* Hastings House, New York, 1973.

Hansen, Gladys, *San Francisco Almanac.* Chronicle Books, San Francisco, 1975.

Iacopi, Robert, *Earthquake Country.* Lane Books, Menlo Park, California, 1971.

James, Marquis, and Bessie, R., *Biography of a Bank.* Harper & Row, New York, 1954.

Johnson, Paul C., *San Francisco.* Kodansha International Ltd., Tokyo, 1976.

Johnson, William Weber, *The Forty-Niners.* Time-Life Books, New York, 1974.

Kahn, Edgar M., *Cable Car Days.* The Scrimshaw Press, Oakland, 1976.

Kerouac, Jack, *On the Road.* Penguin Books Ltd., Harmondsworth, Middlesex, 1974.

Lewis, Oscar, *San Francisco: Mission to Metropolis.* Howell-North Books, Berkeley, 1966.

Longstreet, Stephen, *The Wilder Shore.* W. H. Allen, London, 1969.

McDowell, Jack, ed., *San Francisco.* Sunset Books, Lane Publishing Co., Menlo Park, California, 1977.

Meltzer, David, ed., *Golden Gate, Interviews with Five San Francisco Poets.* Wingbow Press, 1976.

Muscatine, Doris, *Old San Francisco.* G. P. Putnam's Sons, New York, 1975.

Roberts, Steven V., *Eureka!* Quadrangle, The New York Times Book Co., 1974.

Rockwell, Robert, ed., *The Cable Cars of San Francisco.* San Francisco Public Utilities Commission, San Francisco, n.d.

Smith, David, and Luce, John, *Love Needs Care.* Little Brown and Company, Boston, 1971.

Thomas, Gordon, and Morgan-Witts, Max, *Earthquake.* Souvenir Press, London, 1971.

Tytell, John, *Naked Angels.* McGraw-Hill Book Company, New York, 1976.

Walker, Franklin, *San Francisco's Literary Frontier.* University of Washington Press, 1970.

Acknowledgements and Picture Credits

The editors wish to thank the following for their valuable assistance: Robert A. Burchell, University of Manchester; Carolyn de la Plain, London; William Donaldson, London; Susan Goldblatt, London; David Sinclair, Peterborough, Cambs.; Giles Wordsworth, London.

Quotes on pages 24 and 27 from *On the Road* by Jack Kerouac, published 1957, reproduced by permission of Viking Press, New York.
Sources for pictures in this book are shown below.

Credits for the pictures from left to right are separated by commas; from top to bottom by dashes. All photographs are by Jay Maisel except: Pages 12, 13—Map by Hunting Surveys Ltd., London (Silhouettes by Anna Pugh). 22—Photo by Fred Kaplan. 23—Photo by Michael Zagaris. 44—J. R. Eyerman, courtesy collection Carl Shaefer Dentzel. 46—Courtesy The Bancroft Library, University of California, Berkeley. 47—California Historical Society, Fine Arts Collection, San Francisco. 50, 51, 52—Courtesy The Bancroft Library, University of California, Berkeley. 53—Courtesy The New York Historical Society. 59—Wells Fargo Bank History Room, San Francisco. 60, 61, 71—Courtesy The Bancroft Library, University of California, Berkeley. 93—California Historical Society Library, San Francisco. 96, Top Left—Wells Fargo Bank History Room, San Francisco. 126—Wells Fargo Bank History Room, San Francisco. 155—California Historical Society Library, San Francisco. 170, 172, 173—Wells Fargo Bank History Room, San Francisco.

Index

Numerals in italics indicate a photograph or
drawing of the subject mentioned.

Colour reproduction by Irwin Photography Ltd., at their Leeds Studio.
Filmsetting by C. E. Dawkins (Typesetters) Ltd., London, SE1 1UN.
Printed and bound in Italy by Arnoldo Mondadori, Verona.